Photo by Bill Reynolds.

RIPPED 3

The Recipes, The Routines & The Reasons

by Clarence Bass

Continues the
Journey
Begun by
RIPPED
RIPPED2 and
THE LEAN ADVANTAGE

Clarence Bass' **RIPPED**™ Enterprises
Albuquerque, New Mexico

ISBN 0-9609714-3-2

DEDICATION

To my wife, Carol, with love. She enriches my life in countless ways.

Sixth Printing, 2003

Published by Clarence Bass' Ripped Enterprises
528 Chama, N.E.
Albuquerque, New Mexico 87108
U.S.A.

RIPPED is the trademark of Clarence and Carol Bass.

Library of Congress catalog card number: 80-81446.

ISBN 0-9609714-3-2.

Composition by Graphics One
Albuquerque, New Mexico

Manufactured by Thomson-Shore, Inc.
Dexter, Michigan, U.S.A.

Photographs on front and back cover by *Guy Appelman*.

ACKNOWLEDGMENTS

Guy Trucano patiently typed each section of my manuscript through many revisions. For months on end, we were the only ones who knew how the book was progressing. Thanks for sticking with me, Guy.

Thanks to doctoral candidate Kay Steffens and her boss, Dr. Hemming Atterbom, of the University of New Mexico Human Performance Laboratory for cheerfully measuring my body composition at regular intervals over the last three years. They contributed to this book by helping me stay on track.

Dave Prokop edited this book as he did *Ripped 2*. His writing expertise combined with a knowledge of both the running and bodybuilding fields made him the perfect editor. He did another superb job, adding greatly to the flow and readability of my manuscript.

Carole Wright, Deb Jones and "Golden Fingers" Harriet Moldov of Graphics One did the artwork, typesetting and paste-up to prepare my manuscript in camera-ready form for Thomson-Shore, Inc., the fine company which has printed all of my books. Their collective skill will be evident as you turn from page to page.

My two most faithful correspondents, dedicated endurance and strength athlete Richard Winett, Ph.D., a professor of psychology at Virginia Polytechnic Institute and State University, and Roy Rose, a teacher, singer, weight trainer and keen observer of the bodybuilding scene from Australia, will be surprised to find themselves mentioned here. Nevertheless, I want to acknowledge that the constant interchange of ideas they provide has been invaluable.

As always, I deeply appreciate the opportunity given me by Joe Weider to communicate with the worldwide readership of his *Muscle & Fitness* magazine.

Finally, I thank my 14-year-old son, Matt, for occasionally testing my recipes with his supersensitive palate and for being quiet again so I could concentrate on yet another book.

WARNING

The information in this book is intended for people in good health. Anyone with medical problems — especially hypertension or vascular disease — should see a doctor before starting a diet and exercise program. Individuals over 40 who haven't been exercising should consult a doctor, whatever their state of health.

Invariably, if you are out of shape and want to start training, follow the advice of the American Medical Association: "Start *slowly* and increase the vigor and duration of the activity as your fitness improves."

CONTENTS

INTRODUCTION: Why Ripped 3?

I put all I know into every book. I drain my cup dry, so to speak, thinking I've said it all. About two years later, however, I find my storehouse of information full again. To my surprise and delight, there's more, lots more, to tell bodybuilders — and others, too —about the sensible way to achieve and maintain a strong, healthy, lean body.

In late 1979, I was enthusiastic about telling the story of my initial reduction to 2.4 percent body fat and my victories in National Master's physique competition. The result was *Ripped*. I held nothing back. I divulged everything — the diet, the training, the good and bad of steroids, everything! I thought book writing was out of my system once and for all.

But it wasn't. I continued to train and study, and by 1982 my reservoir of knowledge was again overflowing. I had greatly refined my diet and training techniques. For example, I had added aerobic exercise and hard-day, easy-day training to my repertoire. Significantly, I had not only learned how to eat and exercise to become lean, I had learned how to *stay* that way — something of great interest to almost everyone. I poured out all of my new-found knowledge in *Ripped 2*. I was spent again.

But, lo and behold, by the time 1984 came around, I realized that over the last few years I had written some 50 question-and-answer columns that had appeared in Joe Weider's magazine, *Muscle & Fitness*. They were filled with important material — really significant developments such as the body fat setpoint theory, leanness and life span, alternative training to spread the stress of fat-burning exercise — which didn't deserve to be relegated to some dusty stack of old magazines or, worse, the garbage can. I couldn't let that happen. So I organized all the columns, edited and updated, into 16 chapters of *The Lean Advantage*.

Well, by then I had decided that, so long as I stayed enthusiastic about eating and training properly and hungry for new knowledge, my cup would find a way of being replenished. And I was correct, because two years later, in 1986, I had accumulated several thousand pages of training diaries filled with (among other things) detailed information on every meal and snack I'd consumed since 1980. If I put it in my mouth, it was recorded there in the diaries. By then I had also realized that people weren't satisfied with just reading about my overall diet philosophy and getting a few sample menus; they wanted details and variety. That's what I provide in the first half of *Ripped 3:* "The Recipes."

It took several months, but I analyzed the meals in my diaries and came up with 22 basic meal plans, broken down into breakfast, lunch and dinner. There aren't more recipes because uniform eating is one of my secrets for staying lean.

Of course, I couldn't let it go at just listing recipes — I'm a lawyer, you know; I had to explain the good and bad points of each meal. And this, it turns out, is probably the most important part of *Ripped 3,* because these explanations actually provide a whole nutritional philosophy which will enable you to accomplish what you want — namely, build muscle and stay lean. In other words, what these explanations offer is the essence of the Ripped nutritional approach. You'll see you don't have to starve yourself to stay lean; you just have to eat intelligently!

The second half of the book deals with training. Some think of me as primarily an expert on the nutritional aspects of getting ripped, but training is really my first love. I've been at it for about 35 years, and while it's true that proper eating is essential to success in bodybuilding, exercise has always been my top priority. As you'll soon see, it's the most important factor in getting ripped.

Two exciting topics dominate Part Two of this book, "The Routines." One is the aerobics problem faced by bodybuilders.

The latest research shows that aerobic exercise is a two-edged sword: bodybuilders need its fat-burning benefits, but if they overdo it, they end up losing hard-earned muscle tissue as well as fat. Unfortunately, I've experienced this problem firsthand.

Here, as in my other books, I let you, the reader, learn from my mistakes. I give you detailed guidelines and specific aerobic routines for losing fat without losing muscle. And I give you the reasons as well.

The other topic we deal with in detail in Part Two is the periodization approach to training. Periodization — or training in cycles of increasing intensity and decreasing volume, with the cycles

10

consisting of several distinct phases or "periods" — has been used by Soviet and other eastern European athletes since the 1960s. But it didn't start to catch on with American athletes until the mid-1970s, and even then only in a small way. Moreover, most bodybuilders have never heard of periodization. I thought they'd benefit from learning about it, however. That's why the training portion of this book is devoted in large part to explaining, in detail, how periodization can be adapted to meet the needs of bodybuilders.

You see, I'm convinced that periodization is an almost foolproof way for bodybuilders to avoid sticking points and keep gaining month after month, year after year. After you read this book and put the periodization routines in it to work in your own training program, I think you'll share my enthusiasm. Periodization is simply the best way to train.

Well, my cup is bone dry again. I trust it's only temporary. In the meantime, I hope you'll benefit from *Ripped 3* as much as I enjoyed writing it. Get ripped!

This photo was taken by Bill Reynolds the day after I won the Most Muscular Man Award at the Past-40 Mr. USA Contest.

Bill Reynolds snapped this photo in 1982 when *Ripped 2* was published.

John Balik photographed me in his Santa Monica Studio right before *The Lean Advantage* was released.

Here's one of my latest photos, taken by Guy Appelman in my gym at Ripped
Enterprises. I'm 48. My body fat, as measured by the University of New
Mexico Human Performance Laboratory, is 2.8%.

Photo by Guy Appelman.

PART ONE

The Recipes

PART ONE: THE RECIPES

BRIEFLY, WHAT IS THE RIPPED DIET?

It evolved from the diet I followed to reduce my body fat to 2.4 percent and win my class in the Mr. America Past 40 and Mr. USA Past 40 contests; in the latter contest I also won the Best Abdominals, Best Legs and Most Muscular awards. Using this diet, I reduced my body fat to three percent or lower in each of the last eight years and maintained an average body fat level of about four percent.

That's low! Top marathon runners, as a group probably the leanest athletes on earth, carry about six percent body fat. And exercise physiologists say the rock-bottom essential fat level in males is about three percent (with men in the 40-49 age category averaging about 25 percent). During 1985, the year I turned 48, my high was 4.9 percent and my low was 2.8!

Since the details of my diet are spelled out in *Ripped*, *Ripped 2* and *The Lean Advantage*, I'll only summarize the high points here.

In a nutshell, my approach is to eat whole foods the way they are grown — nothing removed or added. I stress unprocessed foods because they provide lots of chewing, tasting and stomach-filling satisfaction without supplying too many calories.

The other side of the coin is that I avoid calorie-dense foods, i.e., foods which contain a lot of calories in a small volume. Highly refined foods such as sugar, white flour and oil have the natural bulk removed. They provide calories without filling you up; thus, they encourage overeating.

I've found you avoid almost all calorie-dense foods if you eat only natural, unprocessed foods. Best of all, you avoid overeating and become lean.

So I prefer foods that are satisfying and filling without providing too many calories. Foods high in fiber accomplish this best. High-fiber foods are almost always low in calories. They fill you up before you consume more calories than you need. They make you chew your food and eat slower. Unlike calorie-dense foods, they give your appetite control mechanism time to signal your brain that you've had enough to eat before you overeat! Whole grains, fruits and vegetables are the best source of dietary fiber. So they're the backbone of my diet.

But the Ripped diet also is balanced with foods from the milk and meat groups. However, in a departure from the traditional bodybuilder's diet, beef is used primarily as a flavoring agent, not as a main course. For protein, I rely on low-fat milk products, along with nuts, beans, a few eggs, and occasionally fish or chicken.

For those interested in the overall picture, the Ripped diet is high in carbohydrate, low in fat, with a moderate amount of protein.

You'll enjoy the Ripped diet. It's not a crash diet or a diet you can tolerate only the last few weeks before a contest. It's a comfortable diet that makes you feel satisfied and never leaves you hungry. That's why it works so well. It's the healthiest, most effective and pleasant way to become lean and stay lean.

Ice Cream is one of my favorite foods, but it's calorie-dense. I only have a small portion or two on weekends. *Photo by Guy Appelman.*

ABOUT THE RECIPES

The recipes put the Ripped diet principles into practice. They illustrate the type of meals that make you feel full and satisfied without making you fat.

Read all the recipes and what we say about them. That's because each recipe is explained and analyzed so you'll know what makes it work. If there's a possible compromise that will make a meal taste better, we make that clear as well. Each recipe included here was carefully selected to present one or more special message. In addition, the recipes are cumulative; they build on each other. For example, nonfat yogurt is discussed early in the recipes, and then it's included many more times, but without further comment. So, to get full benefit from the recipes, read Part One of this book from start to finish.

It's also important to understand that the recipes are taken from my training diaries; most of them are geared to my needs. The portions are what I eat when I want to lose about one pound a week. I eat slightly more to maintain my body weight. You'll probably require more food or less, depending on your size, body composition, activity level and goals. I've included the total calories in each meal, as well as the calories in each ingredient, so you can make the adjustments you desire.

Adjust the portions to suit yourself, but please don't restrict your calorie intake too severely. Don't rush things. Remember what I said in *Ripped 2*: "Don't try to lose more than one pound of fat a week. Reduce your calorie consumption *slightly*. Increase your calorie expenditure *slightly*." If you're impatient and try to lose faster, you defeat your purpose in three ways: 1) your metabolism slows down to save energy; 2) you lose muscle tissue; and 3) you get hungry and binge.

To help you get started, please note that a moderately active man burns 14 to 16 calories a day for each pound of body weight. An inactive man burns 12 to 14 calories per pound, while a very active man burns 16 to 18 calories. This gives you a formula for calculating how many calories you need to maintain your body weight.

But, in addition to activity level, the number of calories you

One of the biggest mistakes people make is rushing the reducing process. Don't try to lose more than one pound of fat a week. *Photo by Bill Reynolds.*

burn is strongly influenced by how lean you are. That's because most of the food you eat is burned by your muscles. So women, who naturally have less muscle and more fat than men, will burn somewhat fewer calories than these guidelines suggest. They should adjust these figures downward about 20 percent — but no more.

To show you how this operates, I'll use myself as an example. I weigh about 160 pounds, and I'm very active. Therefore, my predicted daily maintenance calorie level is approximately 2,720 (160 x 17). To lose one pound of fat (about 3,500 calories) in a week, I must create a daily caloric deficit of 500 calories (7 x 500 = 3,500).

The best way to accomplish this is eat less *and* exercise more. Accordingly, I'd reduce my maintenance calorie level by 250 calories, bringing it down to 2,470 (2,720 less 250) — just about the caloric intake if you eat three meals and two snacks each day from the recipes included. And I'd burn the rest of the 500 calories by increasing my activity level by 250 calories. Walking three miles each day would more than do it, because a person who weighs 160 pounds burns about 88 calories walking one mile. (A heavier person would burn more calories and a lighter person fewer.) Note that both the calorie reduction and the activity increase are slight. Again, that's the best way to take off fat and keep it off.

Even though I present calorie guidelines to help you adjust the recipes to your needs, I don't want you to become a calorie counter. I rarely count calories myself. If it wasn't for writing books and my magazine column, I probably wouldn't know my caloric intake. Calories do count, but what you eat is more important for lifelong weight control. If you stick to the type of food included in the recipes (and also exercise regularly), your natural appetite control mechanism will do the counting for you. You'll automatically eat the number of calories you need — and no more.

You'll find the recipes we've given you are easy to prepare. That's because they're what my wife calls "simple-to-cook" recipes. Simple, easy-to-fix meals suit our lifestyle. Our days are busy and active. We don't have a lot of time to spend cooking. These recipes work out great, because they're time-efficient, and the plain, simple foods keep us lean and healthy. They'll do the same for you.

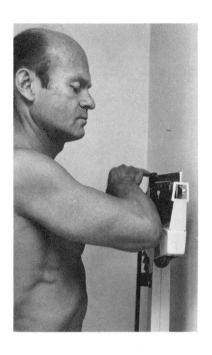

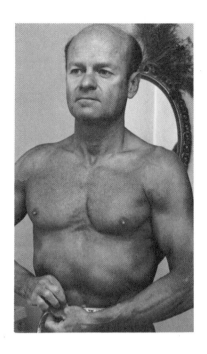

First thing in the morning, I weigh myself, measure my waist and record the results in my diary. Week-to-week changes are more important than what happens day-to-day. That's because eating and activity tend to fall into weekly patterns. For example, most people eat more loosely on the weekend and, therefore, weigh more on Monday and Tuesday. For that reason, your weight on the same day of the previous week is usually more significant than whether you gained or lost from the day before. If your weekly trend is up or you're not losing at the desired rate, a change is probably in order. Keeping careful records puts you in control. You learn how your body responses to specific foods and exercise, and fine tuning to stay on track is much easier. *Photos by Guy Appelman.*

23

Again, I urge you to read all the recipes and the accompanying explanations. Try as many of the recipes as you can. Get comfortable with the Ripped eating style, and don't hesitate to experiment and make changes. Use the recipes here to learn how to alter other recipes. Before you know it, you'll be creating Ripped recipes all your own.

BREAKFAST

MY OLD RELIABLE

	Calories
1 cup cooked whole grains (oat groats, wheat, rye, barley, millet or rice)	approx. 200
1/2 ounce raw unsalted sunflower seeds	80
1/2 ounce raisins	40
1 tablespoon milk-and-egg protein powder	35
1 sliced banana (5 ounces)	120
1 chopped apple (6 ounces)	90
1 cup skimmed milk (1/2% milkfat)	90
Sprinkling of cinnamon	trace
Total Calories	655

If you're wondering, oat groats are hulled whole oats. You can find them and other whole grains in most health food stores and some supermarkets. Cook the grain according to the instructions on the package, but make sure you leave out the salt, butter or oil that are often suggested. If you like, you can add more water to reduce calories. Grain takes about 45 minutes to cook, so prepare enough for several days and store it in the refrigerator.

I usually combine three different grains in one batch. Oats, rye and barley make a good combination. I use three cups of combined grains and eight cups water. Bring the water to a boil, add the grains and let simmer for about 45 minutes or until all the water is absorbed. This makes enough for about nine servings.

Measure out one cup of cooked grain, then add the other ingredients. Be sure to weigh the seeds and raisins (you can purchase an inexpensive food scale at any health food store), because they're the high-calorie ingredients in this recipe.

Comment

It's easy to come up with many enjoyable variations of this recipe that will change the taste or texture of the cereal without

25

This is how oat groats and other whole grains are usually packaged. Whole grains are a staple of my diet. They're a first class example of the bulky, unprocessed foods that fill you up without giving you too many calories. *Photo by Guy Appelman.*

materially altering the nutrients or calories.

As a substitute for sunflower seeds and raisins, I sometimes use an ounce of Raisin Bran, Bran Buds or some other ready-to-eat bran cereal. Of course, most ready-to-eat cereals have added sugar and salt, but a little sugar and salt is acceptable when it adds to your eating pleasure. Don't get carried away, however. Be sure to check the label for ingredients to see *exactly* what you're getting.

You'll find many other similar compromises in my recipes — all designed to make it easier to stick to a good diet plan. Few people can stick to a diet they don't enjoy, and it's not necessary.

Other unsalted nuts and dried fruits can also be substituted for the sunflower seeds and raisins. For example, I like peanuts, chopped almonds or cashews combined with chopped dates or dried apricots. Remember, however, that nuts and dried fruits are concentrated calorie foods, and should be eaten in measured amounts. Stick to the proportions suggested. Add just enough to provide extra taste and crunch without upping the calories more than necessary.

(Top Left) I cook a big batch of grains, enough to last for about a week, and store it in the refrigerator.

(Top Right) I measure a cup of cooked grains as the base ingredient for my cereal. A set of measuring cups will come in handy on many of the recipes.

(Left) It's a good idea to weigh calorie-dense foods such as seeds or nuts. Here I'm weighing the raisins for my favorite cereal recipe. An inexpensive food scale can be purchased at any health food store and many super markets. *Photos by Guy Appleton.*

27

Almost any fruit can be substituted for the banana or apple. I especially like pears, peaches and nectarines. Berries (such as strawberries, blueberries and raspberries) are also good. Apricots, plums, prunes and oranges are other tasty choices.

The milk-and-egg protein powder serves a twofold purpose. It adds extra nutrients but, equally important, it gives the cereal extra sweetness. I market my own brand of protein powder — it's a delicious protein/carbohydrate mixture fortified with vitamins and minerals. So I'd encourage you to use it. But any good-tasting milk-and-egg protein powder is fine.

If you like a thick, creamy texture to your cereal, try substituting plain, nonfat yogurt for the skimmed milk. I especially like a half-and-half mixture of skimmed milk and yogurt.

This cereal tastes delicious hot or cold. On cold winter mornings, I like to pop it into the microwave for three or four minutes and enjoy it piping hot. In case you're wondering, microwave cooking, according to the *University of California, Berkeley Wellness Letter,* preserves more nutrients than conventional cooking

I've made this cereal so many times I could do it in my sleep. I never get tired of it. *Photo by Guy Appelman.*

28

methods because it's so fast and requires no added water. As you'll see, I use the microwave oven often.

Finally, a number of simple changes can be made to add or cut calories. First, simply increase or reduce all the ingredients proportionately. This is best because all the flavor and eating enjoyment is preserved. But if you want to change the calorie content without affecting volume, the amount of sunflower seeds and raisins (the most concentrated sources of calories) can be increased or decreased. Actually, you'll find this cereal is delicious even without the seeds or raisins.

I guarantee that you'll like my cereal. Although I've had it hundreds of times, I never get tired of it. The only complaint I've ever had is that there's simply too much to eat. Some problem!

CREAMY OATMEAL

	Calories
1/2 cup dry rolled oats (regular, not instant)	165
1 cup water	—
1/2 ounce raw, unsalted sunflower seeds	80
1/2 cup plain, nonfat yogurt (calories vary by brand)	50
1 tablespoon milk-and-egg protein powder	
(see "My Old Reliable" recipe)	35
1 ounce raisin bran cereal	90
1 sliced banana (5 ounces)	120
2 ounces fresh strawberries	21
Total Calories	561

Combine oats, water and sunflower seeds; mix well. Cover and place in microwave oven for two minutes or until water is absorbed. Remove from oven and stir in yogurt, protein powder and raisin bran cereal. Top with bananas and strawberries.

Comment

If you'd prefer not to use ready-to-eat cereal, substitute two tablespoons of wheat bran, one tablespoon of wheat germ and one-half ounce of raisins. Add them before heating. When I'm really hungry, I have the whole works: bran, wheat germ, raisins *and* ready-to-eat cereal. That combination adds only 100 calories or so, and gives the oatmeal lots of body.

Other fruits can be substituted for the banana or strawberries, but those two are my favorites on oatmeal. When fresh strawberries are not in season, I substitute one ounce of frozen, sweetened strawberries.

As in the case of "My Old Reliable" recipe, the easiest way to alter the caloric content is by adding or subtracting sunflower seeds or raisins.

You'll need a big bowl for this tasty cereal.

SUNDAY MORNING PANCAKES

		Calories
1/2 cup whole wheat pancake mix		200
1/2 cup skimmed milk (1/2% milkfat)		45
1 large egg		82
1/2 tablespoon vegetable oil		63

Topping:

2/3 cup nonfat yogurt	(calories vary by brand)	67
1 ounce fruit spread		35
1 chopped apple (6 ounces)		90
	Total Calories	582

This recipe makes three or four huge pancakes.

Combine the mix, milk, egg and oil, and mix until batter is fairly smooth. Pour the batter in a hot, nonstick or lightly oiled skillet, and bake. Turn only once, browning on both sides. In other words, follow the instructions on the pancake mix box, but use skimmed milk and reduce the oil. By using skimmed milk and less oil, you reduce the fat and calorie content considerably.

Comment

Most health food stores stock whole wheat pancake mix, but if you can't find whole wheat mix, use Aunt Jemima or any other enriched flour mix. My wife Carol adds two tablespoons of wheat bran and one tablespoon of wheat germ to the Aunt Jemima mix. This adds a few extra calories, but the extra fiber and nutrients are well worth it.

In place of syrup, blend the yogurt, fruit spread and chopped apple into a nutritious, low-calorie topping. Fruit spread is available in most health food stores; it's made from fruit only and contains no sugar, corn syrup or honey. I use Mellow brand fruit spread made in England. It comes in seven flavors — strawberry, blackberry, raspberry, black currant, apricot, orange and mixed fruit — and has only 35 calories per ounce. That's about one-third the calories in regular jelly or jam.

If your health food store doesn't carry Mellow brand, they probably have something similar. Be careful, however. Some of the "no-sugar" spreads are sweetened with honey, and others are extremely concentrated. The result is that there's little, if any, calorie reduction.

In a pinch, you can use one of the low-sugar Smucker's spreads that are available almost everywhere. They contain about half the calories of regular jelly or jam. They don't taste as good as the "fruit only" spreads, however.

I love these pancakes, but there's one major drawback with them. Pancake mix is loaded with sodium — more than 1000 milligrams, or one gram, per half-cup of mix (the sodium is found in the baking soda or sodium bicarbonate listed in the ingredients). Still, that amount of sodium is acceptable on occasion, especially in an otherwise low-sodium diet. But, obviously, you wouldn't want to consume this much sodium the last few days before a contest or photo session. I've seen bodybuilders carb-up on pancakes a few hours before prejudging. Don't make that mistake!

This recipe also makes great waffles. Simply increase the oil to one tablespoon so the waffles will crisp up better. The extra oil adds about 63 calories; therefore, you may want to reduce the

Blackberry is my favorite fruit spread.

Check the ingredients on the label, because some "no sugar" spreads are sweetened with honey, which is no better than sugar. Look for the calorie content too, because some fruit spreads are so concentrated that there's little, if any, calorie reduction.
Photos by Guy Appelman.

topping somewhat.

You'll never know you're watching your calories when you enjoy these pancakes or waffles. They'll turn your Sunday morning breakfast into a feast fit for Louis Cyr or Diamond Jim Brady. The difference is that they won't give you a waistline like those two old-time gluttons sported.

FRENCH TOAST

	Calories
3 slices whole wheat bread	270
1 large egg	82
1/3 cup skimmed milk (1/2% milkfat)	30

Topping:

1/2 cup plain, nonfat yogurt	(calories vary by brand)	50
1 ounce fruit spread (see pancake recipe)		35
1 chopped nectarine		90
	Total Calories	557

Mix egg and milk well. Coat the bread with the mixture and cook in a nonstick or lightly oiled pan until both sides are crispy brown. Top with a mixture of yogurt, fruit spread and chopped nectarine. If nectarines aren't in season, use any other fruit you

I eat plenty of whole grain bread. It's a good diet food. Skip the butter and jelly and you can eat all you want without getting fat. This was proven by an study at Michigan State University. Researchers had slightly obese young men eat 12 slices of high-fiber bread each day; otherwise they were free to eat as much as they desired. The subjects lost on an average 19.4 pounds. The reason: the bread filled their stomachs and satisfied them before they ate too many calories. *Photo by Guy Appelman.*

33

like. My regular standbys are apples and bananas, because they're always available.

If you're concerned about cholesterol, substitute two or three egg whites for the whole egg I use.

Comment

This is one of my weekend favorites. French toast is easier to make than pancakes or waffles. It's also lower in sodium.

Some varieties of whole wheat bread have fewer calories than I've shown. Pritikin bread, for example, is very low in calories. The problem is that these low-calorie breads don't meet my taste standards. Since I eat most of my bread plain, I want a bread that's thick, chewy and has plenty of flavor. One of my favorites is "Bran For Life," a high-fiber, protein-rich bread made by the Food For Life Baking Company in Los Angeles. Tasty bread adds greatly to eating pleasure and makes this French toast especially good.

Because of its fiber content and bulk, bread is a good diet food. In other words, bread isn't the place to cut calories — whether you're making French toast or anything else. Many delicious varieties of whole wheat bread are available. Look around and select those you like best.

THE ALL-AMERICAN

	Calories
2 large poached eggs, cooked without butter or oil	164
2 slices whole wheat toast	180
1 ounce fruit spread (see pancake recipe)	35
2 shredded wheat biscuits topped with:	180
1/2 cup skimmed milk (1/2% milkfat)	45
1 medium sliced peach	40
Total Calories	644

Comment

I have eggs no more than once or twice a week because of the

34

cholesterol content. When I do have eggs, however, I follow the advice of cardiologist-author-runner Dr. George Sheehan, who says if you're going to have one egg you might as well have two.

Apparently, beyond a certain point, additional cholesterol has no effect on blood levels. Once you have reached 300 milligrams of cholesterol — about the amount in one large egg — more cholesterol has no practical consequences. Putting it another way, the 600 milligrams of cholesterol in two eggs is not likely to increase the level in your blood any more than the cholesterol in one egg.

Besides, Frank Zane, a three-time Mr. Olympia winner who has studied nutrition extensively, says an egg is the best thing you can put in your mouth. Except for the cholesterol factor, he may be correct.

Eggs are the standard by which all protein sources are judged; they contain all of the essential amino acids and are roughly 96 percent assimilable. Eggs also contain vitamins A, D, E, B_2, niacin and biotin, plus copper, iron, phosphorus and unsaturated fats. About the only essential nutrient they lack is carbohydrate.

Whatever the pros and cons, I enjoy having eggs occasionally. It's hard to beat the flavor blend of egg and bread. That combination (eggs and bread), plus fruit spread, and cereal with milk and fruit makes a mighty satisfying breakfast.

MATT'S BREAKFAST MALT

	Calories
1 cup skimmed milk (1/2% milkfat)	90
1 large egg	82
1 banana (5 ounces)	120
2 tablespoons milk-and-egg protein powder (see "My Old Reliable" recipe)	70
2 slices whole grain cinnamon-raisin toast	190
Total Calories	552

Comment

When my 14-year-old son Matt asks me to prepare a quick

breakfast for him, I usually make a high-protein malt and serve it to him with cinnamon-raisin toast. I just put the milk, an egg, a banana and the protein powder in our blender.

It takes about five minutes to make a malt, drink it, and clean the blender afterwards. I know, because I'm a malt drinker from way back. From about age 14, when I started reading Bob Hoffman's articles in *Strength & Health* magazine, until I was out of law school, I had a Hoffman's Hi-Proteen malt for breakfast almost every day. It didn't hurt me, either, because I made steady progress as an Olympic lifter all those years. I still whip up a malt with protein powder — using my own brand now — as a quick substitute for any meal.

If you like a "crunchy" malt — Matt doesn't, but I do — throw one ounce of Kellogg's Bran Buds or some other bran cereal in the blender with the other ingredients. In addition to adding crunch, the cereal adds fiber, which most high protein drinks lack.

Matt's breakfast malt sure brings back memories! All those years when my blender was about the most used appliance in our house. You know, it still comes in pretty handy on occasion.

THE WORKS

	Calories
1 cup cooked whole grains (see "My Old Reliable" recipe)	approx. 200
1/2 ounce raisins	40
1/2 ounce unsalted peanuts	80
2 tablespoons milk-and-egg protein powder (see "My Old Reliable" recipe)	70
1 ounce fruit spread (see pancake recipe)	35
1 cup skimmed milk (1/2% milkfat)	90
1 sliced banana (5 ounces)	120
1 chopped apple (6 ounces)	90
1 chopped nectarine	90
1/3 cup nonfat yogurt (Calories vary by brand)	30
Sprinkling of cinnamon	trace
Total Calories	845

Comment

When I'm tired and hungry after a really brutal leg workout in the morning, this is what I have. I call it "The Works" because it contains just about everything but the kitchen sink. It fills up two big bowls (who says I don't eat a lot?). This cereal, the morning newspaper and an hour's rest make me feel like a new man.

Crown this mixture with a few dollops of yogurt and sprinkle with cinnamon. Hide the fruit spread in the middle for a taste surprise when you spoon into it.

Ordinarily, I don't eat this much for breakfast, but it sure hits the spot when I do. And as far as calories and health are concerned, this recipe beats the heck out of more traditional breakfast pig-outs such as steak and eggs with hash browns, biscuits and jelly.

LUNCH

THE FAMOUS PEANUT BUTTER LUNCH

Peanut Butter Sandwich:		**Calories**
2 slices whole wheat bread		180
1 ounce peanut butter (no sugar, salt or oil added)		172
1 cup plain, nonfat yogurt	(calories vary by brand)	100
1 banana (5 ounces)		120
1 large raw carrot		42
	Total Calories	614

Comment

Probably the best known — and least understood — food in my diet is peanut butter. Many find it hard to believe that I can keep my body fat low while eating peanut butter. Their skepticism is well-founded, because peanut butter is loaded with fat and calories. Seventy-five percent of the calories in peanut butter come from fat, and fat has more than twice the calories found in carbohydrate or protein. Putting it another way, a small amount of fatty food like peanut butter contains more calories than a much larger volume of a high-carbohydrate food like potato or a high-protein food like tuna. So peanut butter is a classic example of the calorie-dense foods which should be avoided. Why, then, do I eat peanut butter almost every day?

It's simple. I like peanut butter. Understand, however, that I'm careful how much I eat. I eat peanut butter only in measured amounts. Note that there's only one ounce of peanut butter (approximately two tablespoons) in this recipe. I don't gorge on peanut butter and neither should anyone else. But just as important, foods like peanut butter, which add greatly to eating pleasure, should not be purged from one's diet — even right before a contest.

There's a strong psychological component to eating. It's human nature to crave what you can't have, and craving usually spells doom for dieters.

Geneen Roth talks about compulsive eating in her fascinating book *Feeding the Hungry Heart* (The Bobbs-Merrill Company, 1982). She says diets don't work because they are based on deprivation. She maintains: "A binge is the other side of a diet; it's built into it; it's inevitable. For every diet there is an equal and opposite binge." Roth would've hit the nail squarely on the head if she had said that diets don't work *when* they're based on deprivation.

Predictably, I've had the most trouble controlling my diet on the rare occasions when I've restricted myself severely. An experience I had a few years ago shows what's likely to happen after a period of dietary deprivation.

I ended my peaking period with two photo sessions spread several weeks apart, the first at home in Albuquerque and the second in Las Vegas, Nev. Even though I brought Bill Reynolds, the editor-in-chief of *Muscle & Fitness* and an excellent physique photographer, to Albuquerque to photograph me, the results were disappointing. I looked puffy even though my body fat was down to a rock-bottom 2.4 percent. I was holding too much water under my skin.

Not wanting to waste the peak I'd worked months to achieve, I arranged a second photo session two weeks later in Las Vegas, where the NPC National Bodybuilding Championships were taking place. On this occasion Denie Walter, editor of *Muscle Training Illustrated* and also a top photographer, would be shooting the pictures.

In the time between the two photo sessions, I was extra careful about my caloric intake. I wanted to make sure my body fat stayed low. And to solve my water retention problem, I decided — here was the rub! — to dry out before the second photo session. The last two days before the session with Denie, I clamped down hard on my fluid intake.

Restricting my food intake wasn't difficult — actually it was easy. But limiting my water intake bothered me a lot. Simply knowing that I couldn't drink freely made me thirsty. The problem was mainly in my mind, because I didn't dehydrate enough to cause any physical problems. It was just a matter of wanting what I couldn't have.

Eating peanut butter hasn't hurt my physique. Actually, I think it helps because it keeps me satisfied. Of course, I don't gorge on peanut butter. *Photo by John Balik.*

40

The second photo session didn't turn out well, either — this time I was too dried out. But the really telling development was what happened afterward. I went on an eating and drinking binge that lasted more than a month. I gained almost 12 pounds of water and fat, and ended up at my highest body weight in years!

It was a good lesson. I've gone easier on myself since then, and the results have been considerably better. The message is clear: Don't deny yourself the food or drink you really want, including, of course, peanut butter. While you must be careful with calorie-dense foods such as peanut butter, don't try to eliminate them entirely from your diet.

Some Variations on the Original Recipe.

As you might expect, I've experimented with ways to keep my calories under control and still enjoy peanut butter. Here are some tasty variations on my basic peanut butter lunch.

I've already told you about the "fruit only" spread that goes well with pancakes and waffles. That same fruit spread can be used to make a delicious peanut butter and jelly sandwich. Simply reduce the peanut butter in the basic recipe to one tablespoon (approximately one-half ounce) and substitute a half-ounce of fruit spread. Besides creating every kid's favorite sandwich, this switch eliminates about 70 calories! That's because half an ounce of fruit spread has far fewer calories than the peanut butter it replaces — 17.5 calories in the fruit spread versus 86 in the peanut butter.

Another interesting variation is a peanut butter-tofu sandwich. Again, use half an ounce of peanut butter, and add a two-ounce slice of tofu. The tofu adds volume to the sandwich and cuts calories as well. There are only 41 calories in two ounces of tofu.

Tofu (soy bean curd) is low in fat, high in protein and has a nice, bland taste. It blends well with other foods; the combination of peanut butter and tofu is especially good.

Peanut butter and banana is another great combination. Try half an ounce of peanut butter with two or three ounces of banana. Again, this produces a sandwich with fewer calories than a regular peanut butter sandwich.

Recently I've tried eating whole peanuts, roasted but unsalted, in place of peanut butter. I eat the peanuts along with the bread, fruit and yogurt. It's a terrific blend of flavors. I usually have three slices of bran bread, half an ounce of peanuts, an apple and six ounces of yogurt. This gives me less fat and more fiber in my lunch, and also reduces total calories. As a matter of fact, I believe the extra bread in this variation actually makes it a more satisfying lunch than my original peanut butter sandwich.

I don't wolf down the peanuts, however. I eat them one at a time. They last longer that way, and I enjoy them more.

Those who have read my earlier books will notice that I've switched from whole milk yogurt to the nonfat variety. I did that not only to reduce fat and calories, but also because I found a brand of nonfat yogurt (Alta-Dena) that I really like. The health food store where I shop carries plain, nonfat Alta-Dena yogurt which has less than one gram of fat and only 100 calories per cup. Compare that to the 150 or more calories in a cup of whole milk yogurt.

This plain, nonfat yogurt was a real find. Not only do you get fewer calories, but it has a mild flavor that I prefer over the more acidic taste of whole milk yogurt. Nonfat yogurt is now a staple in my diet.

If you try nonfat yogurt, be sure to check the caloric content. It varies from brand to brand. Most nonfat yogurt provides 125 calories or more per cup. In reading the nutritional data on the containers, you'll also notice that low-fat yogurt — as opposed to nonfat varieties — provides more than 160 calories per cup. Of course, *flavored* low-fat yogurt isn't low in calories at all. Flavored low-fat yogurt usually has 225 or more calories per eight ounces. That means it actually belongs in the dessert category.

Finally, there are a number of other ways to change this lunch recipe. These variations don't reduce calories, but they do give your tastebuds something different.

If you want a change from peanut butter, try the other nut butters available in health food stores. Almond butter, sunflower seed butter, sesame seed butter and cashew butter all make delicious sandwiches.

It's also nice to vary the fruit you have with your lunch. In place of banana, try an apple, pear, nectarine or peach, or even a little

42

Plain nonfat yogurt (100 calories to the cup) is another regular item in my diet. It's one of the most versatile foods I know. *Photo by Guy Appelman.*

dried fruit. Go easy on dried fruit, however, because it has a lot of calories packed into a small volume. Dried apricot is my favorite, but dried apple, peach, papaya, pineapple and prunes are also good.

Of course, any number of vegetables — cauliflower, broccoli, green beans, celery, cucumber and turnips (to name a few) — can be substituted for the raw carrot I usually have with this lunch. Tomato is another of my favorites. You can slice it or eat it like an apple. Tomato and nonfat yogurt make a good combination; it's quite similar to the taste of tomato and mayonnaise, but without the extra calories.

Before giving you my next lunch recipe, let me reiterate that peanut butter and other calorie-dense foods shouldn't always be written off as too fattening. Sure, you should monitor your intake of such foods, but don't deny yourself entirely. Tell yourself you can't have these goodies, and you'll want them all the more. You'll crave them. Denial and deprivation are the sure route to diet failure.

So enjoy your peanut butter!

Here's one of the photos taken by Denie in Las Vegas after I reduced my fluid intake. I remember that simply knowing I couldn't drink freely made me thirsty. It was a good lesson.

44

THE BIBLE BREAD SPECIAL

		Calories
6 ounces unleavened sprouted cinnamon/date bread		410
1 cup nonfat yogurt	(calories vary by brand)	100
1 pear (7 ounces)		120
	Total Calories	630

Comment

Unleavened, sprouted bread can be traced back to biblical times. The type I use is made of sprouted wheat, whole pitted dates and ground cinnamon. It has no leavening agent (baking powder, yeast, etc.) to make it rise, and no salt, sugar, oil or flour. Yet it's a rich, moist, chewy bread. If you haven't tried it before, you're in for a treat.

You'll find many varieties of this bread at your health food store. I've had plain wheat, rye and multigrain, as well as those made with added raisins, carrots and, of course, dates. They're all delicious. I even tried sprouted fruitcake bread once. It's good, too — in fact, too good! I didn't buy it again: too many calories.

The calorie count varies from one variety of this bread to the next. As you'd expect, those made with raisins, seeds and other extras are higher in calories than the plain version. Be sure to check the label for ingredients and calorie count.

Bible bread is so substantial, you can easily build a lunch around it. This bread is excellent with yogurt and fruit. I warn you, however, that even the plain varieties contain natural sugars. The sprouting process converts starch into maltose and other natural sweeteners. You'll be tempted to eat more than you should.

You can protect against that by slicing off only what you plan to eat and put the rest back in the refrigerator. This works well for me. With the balance out of sight and reach, six ounces usually satisfies me just fine.

Try Bible bread when you want something special for lunch. I usually have it at home on weekends, but it's good anytime and anywhere.

A TASTE OF TUNA

	Calories
4 slices whole wheat bread, toasted	360
2 ounces water-packed tuna	70
1/4 cup nonfat yogurt (calories vary by brand)	25
1 celery stalk, chopped fine	5
1 ounce tomato, drained and chopped fine	6
2 green onions, chopped fine	5
1/2 ounce dill pickle, chopped fine	trace
1 teaspoon mustard	5
1 packet of Equal (trade name: NutraSweet) low-calorie sweetener — optional	4
1 apple (6 ounces)	90
Total Calories	570

Mix the tuna with the other ingredients, then spread the mixture on the bread. Makes two sandwiches. Eat the apple on the side.

Comment

Good ol' water-packed tuna. Some bodybuilders practically live on it. I read in *Supercut,* the book by Bill Reynolds and Joyce Vedral (Contemporary Books, 1985), that former Mr. America Tim Belknap lunches on water-packed tuna. That's it, nothing but tuna.

It's easy to understand why tuna is so popular with bodybuilders. It's almost pure protein and quite low in calories — seven ounces provides 56 grams of protein and only 254 calories. Still, that's no reason to eat it by the canful! Huge amounts of tuna just clog up your digestive system. Your body simply can't assimilate all that protein at one time. You end up with indigestion and a stomachache.

On the other hand, most people can easily digest the two ounces of tuna included in this recipe. Equally important, a tuna salad sandwich tastes better than straight tuna.

Tuna is almost pure protein and quite low in calories. Still, I only eat it in small amounts. Meat of any kind, eaten in large amounts, causes constipation. *Photo by Bill Reynolds.*

As readers of my books and column know, I eat very little meat of any kind. That's mainly because meat contains little or no fiber and slows the digestion process. My bowels function better without meat. I prefer to use meat as a flavoring agent and not as a main course.

Nevertheless, meat, fish and chicken do add greatly to eating pleasure. As I've said before, eating satisfaction is important to the success of any dietary plan. That's why this tuna salad sandwich and a number of meat dishes are included among my recipes. You'll note, however, that none of the recipes have meat in large amounts.

By the way, let me warn you: This tuna sandwich is very tasty, but it's also high in sodium. Most water-packed tuna has added salt — there's about 310 milligrams of sodium in the two ounces used here. And the salt in the bread (556 mg.), dill pickle (200 mg.) and yogurt (40 mg.) bring the sodium content to a substantial level. So enjoy this sandwich, but not before a contest.

You may be surprised that I use an artificial sweetener in this recipe. I have no health concerns about using Equal. The US Food and Drug Administration and the American Medical Association have determined that unless you suffer from PKU (phenylketonuria) or epilepsy, there are no apparent dangers associated with taking aspartame, the sweetener used in Equal (the trade name is NutraSweet). But if you still have reservations, use fructose, regular sugar, or no sweetener at all.

When I was a kid, my mother made tuna salad for me using mayonnaise and sugar. I still like it that way but, as you can see, I now reduce the calories by using nonfat yogurt and Equal.

I also use Equal in my coffee and occasionally on my cereal and other foods. There is a problem with using low-calorie sweeteners, however. Added sweetness, from sugar or non-caloric sources, tends to stimulate the appetite; therefore, you may eat more than you would otherwise. I'll give you the same advice I give myself regarding low-calorie sweeteners: Use them if you like, but don't overdo it. Also, realize that there's no proof that low-calorie sweeteners are effective in weight control. Still, I believe they do add to eating pleasure, which is important.

A final note: This recipe can easily be turned into a "Taste of

Chicken" or an egg salad sandwich. Simply use two ounces of skinless chicken or a chopped egg in place of tuna.

A LOAF OF BREAD, CHEESE — AND THOU

		Calories
2 slices whole wheat bread		180
1 ounce mozzarella cheese		85
1 sliced tomato		33
1 cup nonfat yogurt	(calories vary by brand)	100
1 baked potato, with skin (6 ounces cooked)		120
1 apple (6 ounces)		90
	Total Calories	608

Comment

In naming this recipe, I took some liberties with the words of the 19th-century English poet Edward FitzGerald: "A jug of wine, a loaf of bread — and thou." Among other things, that famous line makes me think of cheese, and I don't think I'm alone in that reaction. I imagine a picnic lunch on a grassy bank by a babbling brook. Cheese fits right into that setting, don't you think? Anyway, most people like cheese.

Unfortunately, cheese presents some problems. The drawbacks are summed up in the November 1985 issue of the *University of California, Berkeley Wellness Letter*: "[Cheese is] a mixed blessing — high in protein, but also saturated fat, usually full of calcium but also sodium, rich and creamy but loaded with cholesterol." One ounce of cheese has as much fat as a whole cup of milk. In terms of saturated fat and cholesterol, it's worse than most meats.

That's why I usually select mozzarella cheese and eat only a limited amount. Regular mozzarella is lower in fat, sodium and calories than most other cheeses. And it's possible to get partly skimmed varieties which have even less fat and cholesterol, although approximately the same number of calories.

An average slice of the regular variety of mozzarella cheese — approximately the amount in this recipe — contains seven grams

49

of protein, six grams of fat, 105 milligrams of sodium and 85 calories. That makes it about two-thirds fat. But that's still much better than the 80 percent fat in cheddar, American, Swiss or Roquefort, and the 90 percent in cream cheese!

For obvious reasons, it's best to reserve cheese — any kind — for an occasional treat or use it to add flavor to other dishes. Don't make it a main course. Like peanut butter, it's okay to enjoy cheese, but it's a mistake to eat very much.

It doesn't take much time or effort to throw this lunch together. All you have to do is weigh out the cheese, slice the tomato, and bake the potato in the microwave oven. It's a simple meal with a nice blend of flavors.

Or perhaps you identify with the line from Robert Louis Stevenson's *Treasure Island:* "Many's the long night I dreamed of cheese — toasted mostly." If that's the case, toast the bread, lay the cheese on top with some sliced tomato, and put the whole thing in the microwave for a minute or two. *Voila,* you've got a toasted cheese sandwich. If it appeals to you, add some salsa or chopped green chile.

Whichever method of preparation you prefer, this recipe makes a good-tasting sandwich, and with yogurt, fruit and potato, it'll fill you up and make you feel satisfied.

CAROL'S VEGGIE PLATE

		Calories
1 cup nonfat yogurt	(calories vary by brand)	100
1 large baked potato, with skin (7 ounces cooked)		140
1 cup green beans (fresh or frozen)		35
1 large raw carrot		42
1 sliced tomato		36
1 cup sliced cucumber		16
	Total Calories	369

Comment

My wife, Carol, has a gluten intolerance; she can't eat most breads. As a consequence, she's big on vegetables. This is one of her favorite lunches, and the recipe is modified here to fill up a man-sized stomach. She'd have the yogurt, baked potato, green beans... and skip the rest. I'd eat it all.

Carol was a longtime student of the late Nathan Pritikin, who recommended eating raw vegetables all day long to lose weight. This meal illustrates why that works. Vegetables have volume but few calories. They fill you up without making you fat.

I've already told you that nonfat yogurt has become a staple in my diet. It's particularly delicious here. Yogurt complements the taste of most vegetables, including those in this recipe. Eat the yogurt slowly so it will last until the final bite of vegetable.

Some other low-calorie vegetables that Carol and I suggest you try for lunch are squash (all kinds), celery, bell pepper, cabbage, cauliflower, broccoli, green onion and alfalfa sprouts. They're all good with yogurt.

In addition to varying the vegetables, we also suggest that you occasionally skip the yogurt. Instead, have an ounce of low-fat cheese or a hard-boiled egg.

When you're watching your calories like a hawk and you're really hungry, Carol's Veggie Plate is just what the doctor ordered. Try it!

SUPER FRUIT SALAD

	Calories
1 chopped apple (6 ounces)	90
1 sliced banana (5 ounces)	120
1 chopped peach (4 ounces)	38
2 ounces fresh strawberries	22
1/2 ounce unsalted raw sunflower seeds or peanuts	80
1 cup nonfat yogurt (calories vary by brand)	100
Sprinkling of cinnamon	trace
1 loaf whole wheat pita bread with sesame seeds (2 ounces)	180
Total Calories	630

Put the chopped fruit and strawberries in a big bowl; add the sunflower seeds or peanuts and the yogurt. Stir to distribute the yogurt throughout the salad. Sprinkle cinnamon on top.

Comment

As is the case with vegetables, you can eat a lot of fruit without getting fat. Fruit is also quite filling and satisfying, especially when combined with yogurt and seeds or nuts. The yogurt gives this fruit salad a creamy consistency, and the seeds or nuts add crunch. Also important, the fat in the seeds or nuts really helps to satiate your appetite, makes the salad "stick with you" longer.

Pita bread originated in the Middle East. It's made with whole wheat, water, sesame seeds, yeast and (usually) salt. It's also known as pocket bread, because it forms a pocket when you open it with a knife. It can be stuffed with your favorite filling, but I usually toast it and eat it plain without a filling. Pita bread is chewier than regular bread, and I find it a perfect complement to this fruit salad.

Like Carol's Veggie Plate, Super Fruit Salad fills you up without filling you out. To reduce the calories, drop one piece of fruit from the recipe, and reduce or eliminate the seeds or nuts.

I particularly enjoy Super Fruit Salad on a hot summer afternoon, but it's good year-round.

WHY I BELIEVE IN UNIFORM EATING

We have now reached the end of the lunch recipes. Before we move on to dinner, let me explain why I place such importance on a uniform eating plan.

Those who have read my previous books know that I usually have peanut butter or peanuts for lunch (the first recipe we gave you in this section). Uniform eating is an important part of my program to stay lean. And I have peanut butter or peanuts for lunch about 85 percent of the time because it's easier to keep track of my calories that way. Like a scientist conducting an experiment, I can follow what's happening to my body better if I'm consistent in my eating. On the other hand, if I whipped up something different every day, I'd be counting calories constantly — and going half-crazy doing it.

Except for Carol's Veggie Plate, the lunch recipes in this book all have about the same number of calories (570 to 630). That's another form of uniform eating. And now that I've given you a variety of lunch recipes to choose from, all with about the same calorie count, you can modify the recipes to suit your tastebuds and caloric needs. As long as you stay aware of what you're doing, you can switch around as much as you like and still keep your calories under control.

The time when I stray from my peanut butter or peanut lunch most often is on weekends and holidays. That's when I pick one of the other lunch recipes included here or prepare something else that appeals to me at the time. Eating different things on weekends and holidays provides enough variety to keep me content; then I'm happy to go back to my regular lunch on Monday.

Now let's look at dinner, where you'll notice my meals vary the most.

DINNER

BROWN RICE & BEANS

	Calories
1 cup cooked brown rice (5-1/2 ounces)	178
1/2 cup pinto beans, cooked fresh or canned without sugar or oil added	140
3 ounces diced carrot	36
2 ounces chopped tomato	12
1 ounce diced bell pepper	6
1/2 cup nonfat yogurt (calories vary by brand)	50
2 tablespoons salsa (no sugar or oil added)	16
2 slices whole wheat bread, toasted	180
Total Calories	618

Precook rice and beans. Combine rice, beans, carrot, tomato, bell pepper, yogurt and salsa in a large bowl; mix well. Cover. Heat in microwave oven for about eight minutes. This length of cooking blends the flavors without taking the crunch out of the bell pepper and carrot. If you prefer the carrot more tender, cook longer.

Comment

This dinner is a perfect illustration of my Ripped eating style: whole, unprocessed foods with no sugar or fat added and no fiber removed. As I say in *Ripped 2,* unless you simply set out to stuff yourself, it's difficult to overeat on a meal like this.

A plateful of rice and beans (one cup rice and one-half cup beans) contains approximately the same number of calories and just as much protein as three ounces of T-bone steak. A plateful of rice and beans, however, is more filling and satisfying than three ounces of T-bone steak. That's because rice and beans are high in complex carbohydrates and fiber, and low in fat. The rice and beans in this recipe contain less than two grams of fat, compared to 31.5 grams in three ounces of T-bone steak! In fact, even when you include the yogurt and bread, this whole meal contains less than five grams of fat. That's why it has so much volume and so few calories.

I know that some people dismiss rice and beans as a low-quality poor man's food. But many traditional cultures around the world derive their protein from a combination of rice and beans. Beans alone have most (although not all) of the essential amino acids. And when they're served with rice or dairy products (as in this case) or a small amount of meat, they build muscle just as well as a T-bone steak. For bodybuilders, therefore, rice and beans are actually better than steak; they provide high-quality protein, and they do it without making you fat.

To save time when I'm going to be making this meal, I cook a big batch of brown rice and store it in the refrigerator. It's easy to do. Use nine cups water and three cups rice. Bring the water to a boil, add rice and then turn the heat down. Cover and let simmer until all the water is absorbed — usually about 45 minutes. This makes enough for about 10 one-cup servings.

I eat whole, unprocessed foods whenever I can. that's why I prefer brown rice. It contains more fiber than white rice. It tastes better, too. *Photo by Guy Appelman.*

Brown rice requires more cooking than the white variety, but it's worth the extra time. White rice is "enriched" just like white bread. This means a few nutrients are put back in after processing, but much of the fiber, fat and other nutrients found in the discarded bran and germ are lost. And white rice has a rather bland flavor compared to the rich, nutty taste of brown rice. Therefore, brown rice has more nutrients and better flavor. The only drawback is that it also has about nine percent more calories.

If you buy dried beans, be sure to soak them in cold water in the refrigerator overnight before cooking, then discard the water. Overnight soaking substantially reduces complex sugars that can't be digested and consequently cause gas and bloating. To further reduce the flatulence problem, discard the water again after cooking. Pre-soaking also cuts down on cooking time, but even after soaking, it takes a long time for beans to cook — 1-1/2 to 2-1/2 hours.

Another problem is that home-cooked beans often spoil in the refrigerator before they're used. If you cook your own beans, I suggest that you make a large batch and freeze some in meal-size containers. This saves cooking time and solves the spoilage problem.

Actually, since fresh beans are such a hassle to prepare and keep, most of the time I use canned beans. I'm careful what kind I buy, however. I look for beans canned with water, salt and spices only — you don't want sugar or oil which will add calories. When sodium is a special concern with me — before a contest or photo session, for example — I buy beans packed with water only, no salt (beans alone are very low in sodium). Generally, however, I don't worry about the sodium in canned beans; they definitely taste better with salt and spices added.

My favorite salsa — Old El Paso Thick 'n Chunky — also has added salt. It's made with tomatoes, green chiles, onions, vinegar and garlic. It's very low in calories, however, because no sugar or oil is added.

As I've said before, the taste of the food is important to the success of any eating plan. The salsa makes this meal; it turns essentially bland rice and beans into a spicy taste treat. Of course, you can make your own salsa without salt. You can also buy salsa

For bodybuilders, rice and beans are actually better than steak; this combination provides high quality protein, and does it without making you fat. *Photo by John Balik.*

with no added salt at a health food store, although you probably won't like it as well as the salted variety.

Actually, I think it's an acceptable trade-off: a little salt — probably not enough to do any harm — in return for convenience and a better tasting meal. Plus, it just may tip the balance between eating this healthy, low-fat way or going back to the fattening fare eaten by most Americans. Let's face it, you won't eat foods you don't like — not for long, anyway.

Personally, I love being able to eat as much rice and beans as I want without getting fat. And with the salt and spices added, I don't feel a bit deprived. Try it. You'll like it!

THE BIG SALAD

	Calories
3 ounces iceberg lettuce, torn into bite-sized pieces	11
3 ounces raw red or green cabbage, shredded	17
1 tomato (5 ounces), cut into small wedges	31
3 ounces peeled cucumber, sliced	12
3 ounces raw yellow squash, cut into bite-size pieces	12
2 ounces chopped bell pepper	13
1 ounce chopped radishes	5
2 hard-cooked eggs, chopped	164
1/2 ounce roasted peanuts, unsalted	80
Dressing:	
1/2 cup nonfat yogurt (calories vary by brand)	50
4 tablespoons vinegar	8
1 packet Equal low-calorie sweetener	4
Sprinkle with pepper to taste	
2 slices whole wheat bread	180
Total Calories	587

Place vegetables in a large salad bowl and toss well. Add chopped egg and peanuts. Toss again. Stir yogurt, vinegar and the sweetener together in a separate bowl. Pour dressing over the salad and toss again. Eat the bread with the salad.

The great thing about salad fixings such as bell pepper is that you can eat, and eat, and eat without getting fat. Beware of the dressing, however. *Photo by Guy Appelman.*

Comment

A number of things make this salad really special. First, the multiple colors — the various shades of green, red and yellow in the vegetables — provide eye appeal. The egg and yogurt add more color, but their main contribution is body. They let you know you're eating something substantial — not just rabbit food (which is the way most people think of vegetable salads). The peanuts provide a delightful crunch.

Because of the fat in the eggs and peanuts, this salad stays in your stomach a long time. You could say that, unlike a plain tossed salad, it sticks to your ribs. I'm sometimes hungry two or three hours after dinner, but that's not the case with this meal.

With most salads, dressing is the problem. That's where the excess calories are concealed. Not so here. The generous amount

59

of yogurt dressing in this recipe contains only 62 calories — five calories per tablespoon. Compare that to the 66 calories in a tablespoon of regular French dressing or the 80 per tablespoon in Thousand Island dressing.

This yogurt dressing also has far fewer calories than the low-calorie dressings sold in supermarkets. For example, there are 15 calories in a tablespoon of low-calorie French dressing and 27 calories in one tablespoon of low-calorie Thousand Island dressing. As a matter of fact, the vinegar-and-pepper dressing I recommended in *Ripped,* my first book, is about the only dressing with fewer calories than the one used here.

This dressing demonstrates beautifully why I use nonfat yogurt so frequently. What other food is so nutritious, versatile, good-tasting — and provides so few calories?

As a matter of fact, The Big Salad is another perfect illustration of my high-volume, low-calorie eating style. During the 1977-'79 period covered in *Ripped,* I had a salad like this for dinner almost every night. It was a key factor in my initial reduction to 2.4 percent body fat.

Actually, when you get right down to it, for a person like me who loves to eat, the really great thing about The Big Salad is that it's so... well, BIG. You can eat, and eat, and eat without getting fat.

QUICK VEGETABLE STEW WITH BEEF

	Calories
1 large (7 ounces cooked) baked potato, chopped into bite-size pieces	185
4 ounces frozen mixed vegetables (corn, green peas, carrots, green beans, and slight amount of salt)	80
2 ounces lean ground beef (raw weight)	100
1/2 cup nonfat yogurt (calories vary by brand)	50
1 cup water	—
Herbs and spices to taste	negligible
2 slices whole wheat bread	180
Total Calories	595

Bake potato in microwave oven one minute per ounce of raw weight. Chop baked potato into bite-size pieces. If ground beef is

60

frozen, thaw in microwave for several minutes. Break beef into small pieces. Combine potato, mixed vegetables, water and seasoning in a casserole dish. Spread beef over the top. Cover. Cook in microwave for about five minutes. Remove from oven and add yogurt. Cover again. Cook in microwave for an additional five minutes or until vegetables are hot and beef is fully cooked. Eat the bread with the stew.

Comment

Some of you, I know, will be shocked at the inclusion of beef in this recipe. Red meat! Has Clarence Bass gone bonkers? Not really. I'm simply facing facts. Red meat makes food taste better. A few ounces of beef turns a bland vegetable dish into a feast.

The beef makes this a meal you'll be happy to eat anytime — not only when you're trying to get cut up for a contest. This recipe and the others in this book make up a diet you'll be content to stay with for a lifetime; they're designed to show you how to eat to stay lean, and enjoy it.

The trick is to use red meat to make food taste better, rather than use it as a main course. Note that this meal contains only two ounces of lean ground beef.

Of course, the reason Americans are now eating less red meat is its high fat and cholesterol content. Meat not only makes you fat, but most experts agree that the fat and cholesterol in it cause damage to the arteries and increases the risk of heart attack and other cardiovascular problems. The dangers can be minimized, however, by eating meat in small quantities and sticking to the leaner cuts.

Believe it or not, fat accounts for more than 70 percent of the calories in choice sirloin, ordinary hamburger, processed meat and sausage. Fat accounts for less than 40 percent of the calories in leaner cuts such as flank steak, lean chuck roast and sirloin tip. Less fat, of course, means fewer calories. That's why I use *lean* ground beef in this stew; the two ounces in this recipe provides only 100 calories, compared to more than 150 you'd get from the same amount of regular ground beef.

Recognizing the drawbacks of fatty meat, the public is demanding leaner varieties and butchers are responding. In addition to ordinary hamburger, the supermarket where Carol and I shop offers ground beef labeled "lean," "extra lean" and "super lean." Because it's available everywhere, I include lean ground beef in this recipe. But if you can find super lean ground beef, buy it. It's more expensive, but well worth it. Not only is it delicious, but it's so lean that when you cook it, almost no drainage fat appears in the pan.

Labeling on beef can be misleading, however. Terms like "extra lean" or "super lean" mean whatever the butcher wants them to mean. There is no mandatory system for describing beef. The beef industry, however, has established its own voluntary standard that calls for "lean" to contain less than 24 percent fat and "extra lean" to have no more than 15 percent. If you have questions about the terminology used where you shop, ask the butcher.

There's another reason, in addition to taste, why it may be a good idea to include red meat in your diet occasionally: it's one of the best sources of iron. The iron in meat is absorbed twice as efficiently as that in vegetables, and meat in the diet makes the iron from other sources more usable.

Iron deficiency is considered one of the most common nutritional problems worldwide. Even in the United States, it's estimated that 10 percent or more of the population suffers from this deficiency. A famous victim was marathoner Alberto Salazar. The surprising decline in performance he suffered in 1983, the year before the Los Angeles Olympics, was diagnosed as the result of an iron deficiency. Women, because of their menstrual periods, often suffer from iron deficiency anemia, commonly called iron-poor blood. Iron in the blood helps to transport oxygen from the lungs to the working muscles. When there's an iron deficiency, muscles lack sufficient oxygen and, consequently, fatigue more quickly.

Heme iron is the form most readily usable by the body. It's found in red meat, poultry and seafood, but not in milk products. About 40 percent of the iron in animal meat or fish is heme iron; the body can assimilate about a third of it. Nonheme iron accounts for the other 60 percent of the iron in meat, and *all* the iron in fruits, vegetables, dried beans, nuts and grain products.

For a time I stopped having beef entirely. But now I eat small portions of super lean beef for its iron content and great flavor. Still, I never have beef as a main course. *Photo by Guy Appelman.*

Your body can absorb — at most — only 10 percent of this form.

So it's probably a good idea for hard-training bodybuilders to include red meat in their diet occasionally — for the iron as well as the taste. Keep the portions small, however. Two or three ounces per serving is about right. Carol and I eat lean beef in two-ounce portions (in other words, the amount included in this recipe). We make patties in this serving size and store them in the freezer for use as needed.

You may also wonder about my use of frozen vegetables. It's mainly a matter of convenience. When I get home in the evening, I'm usually tired and hungry. I don't feel like chopping and cutting fresh vegetables before I eat. Besides, a wonderful variety of frozen vegetables is now available at grocery stores. What's more, many of these vegetables have no added calories from sugar, oil or sauce, and they're packed without salt or only a slight amount of salt.

I selected a common mix of frozen vegetables for this recipe, but you'll find many other frozen vegetable combinations at your supermarket. Two other combinations I especially like — they're even lower in calories than the mix included here — are Italian vegetables and Broccoli Normandy. The Italian vegetable combination includes zucchini squash, cauliflower, carrots, Italian green beans and lima beans. The other combination consists of broccoli, cauliflower and carrots. I enjoy experimenting with different vegetables and vegetable combinations, and I think you will, too.

When buying frozen vegetables, be sure to read the nutritional information on the package. Watch out for added sugar, oil, or sauce; they can contribute far more calories than the vegetables themselves.

Salt, of course, is always a concern for bodybuilders. The nutrition information on the package usually includes sodium content. The mixed vegetables I usually buy contain a slight amount of salt, 15 milligrams per 3.3 ounce serving. That's quite reasonable when you consider that a serving of frozen vegetables prepared with salt usually contains more than 300 milligrams of sodium! Needless to say, before a contest, photo session, or some other special occasion, you'll want to use fresh vegetables or frozen vegetables packed without salt.

Incidentally, if you're worried that frozen vegetables aren't as nutritious as fresh vegetables, you can rest easy. According to the *Tufts University Diet & Nutrition Letter,* the nutrient differences in processed versus fresh vegetables are not as great as you might think. For example, one study showed that the amount of vitamin C remaining in peas after cooking was 44 percent (fresh peas), 39 percent (frozen) and 36 percent (canned). As I've already said, the main thing to watch out for with frozen vegetables is sodium content and added calories in the form of sugar, oil or sauce.

Admittedly, fresh vegetables taste better than frozen. So if you have the time and inclination, by all means use fresh vegetables. This recipe, however, is called "Quick" Vegetable Stew, so we've listed frozen vegetables in the ingredients.

Finally, the meat and vegetables in this meal taste good by themselves, but you still may want to add seasoning. If, like me, you're not experienced with herbs and spices, try something simple like chili, garlic, curry or onion powder. (But don't use garlic salt or onion salt; they're loaded with sodium!) And if you're already a practiced herb and spice user, well, you don't need any help from me.

Bon appetit.

When I go to the supermarket my first stop is usually the frozen vegetable bin. If I'm getting something new, I always check the label for sodium content and added sugar, oil or sauce. *Photo by Guy Appelman.*

BAKED VEGETABLE & FRUIT PLATE

	Calories
1 baked sweet potato (5 ounces cooked)	155
1 baked carrot, sliced into bite-size pieces (6 ounces cooked)	53
6 ounces frozen cut broccoli	45
1 baked pear (7 ounces raw weight)	120
1 raw banana (5 ounces)	120
1 cup nonfat yogurt (calories vary by brand)	100
Add pepper, cinnamon and lemon to taste	negligible
Total Calories	593

Bake the sweet potato, sliced carrot, pear and cut broccoli in a microwave oven until tender. Make sure you turn over and rearrange the food items after half the cooking time to ensure even tenderness. Remove pear from the oven first, because it takes less baking time. Use yogurt as a topping or dip. A dash of pepper and a squeeze of lemon enhances the flavor of broccoli. A sprinkling of cinnamon does the same for baked pear.

Comment

This is another meal which demonstrates how filling, satisfying yet low-calorie vegetables and fruits are; as I've already said, they fill you up without filling you out.

Baking brings out the flavor of fruits and vegetables. Everyone likes baked sweet potato. And when baked, carrots and pears take on a delightful added sweetness.

Broccoli, which the *University of California, Berkeley Wellness Letter* calls "the lean, green nutrition machine," adds more than crunch to this meal. This dark green vegetable is an honest-to-goodness health food. One cup of cut broccoli, which is approximately the amount in this recipe, gives you 140 milligrams of vitamin C, 3800 units of vitamin A, 10 percent of your daily requirement of calcium, eight percent of iron, plus substantial amounts of niacin, thiamine and phosphorus. It's also low in sodium, rich in potassium, provides two grams of fiber... and even five grams of protein! As if all that wasn't enough, the

American Academy of Sciences says broccoli is one of the vegetables that may protect against certain forms of cancer. All these benefits — for only 7-1/2 calories per ounce!

Finally, as was the case with The Big Salad, this meal gives you a lot of food. So you'll need a big appetite when you sit down to eat it.

EGGS NEW MEXICAN

	Calories
2 cups shredded iceberg lettuce	20
2 large eggs, soft-cooked	164
1/2 cup pinto beans, canned without sugar or fat added	140
3 tablespoons green chile salsa (no sugar or fat added)	24
2 slices whole wheat bread	180
1 ear corn on the cob, without butter (8 ounces including cob)	120
Total Calories	648

Soft-cook the eggs with a minimum of oil (I use an egg steamer with just enough oil to keep the eggs from sticking). This recipe calls for a green chile salsa without sugar or fat (two good brands: Old El Paso, Pure & Simple). Stir salsa into the beans and heat. Make a bed of shredded lettuce on plate and place eggs on top. Pour beans and salsa mixture over the eggs. Serve the bread and corn on the cob on the side, without butter.

Comment

This is a lean version of my favorite Mexican dish, Huevos Rancheros. I simply leave out the high-calorie ingredients — oil, cheese and avocado — that are usually in the Mexican egg dish. I also use bread instead of tortillas, because the latter are usually made with white flour and lard.

Eggs New Mexico is *muy bueno.* You'll enjoy it.

One more thing: corn on the cob is sweet, juicy and delicious... without butter. Honest!

WHITE FISH DINNER

	Calories
5 ounces halibut (weight raw)	143
1 cup cooked brown rice (5-1/2 ounces)	178
4 ounces peas, carrots and onions (frozen, with a slight amount of salt in the package)	73
4 tablespoons liquid Butter Buds	24
1/3 cup nonfat yogurt (calories vary by brand)	34
1 tablespoon seafood cocktail sauce (Del Monte)	20
1 tablespoon lemon juice (fresh or from concentrate)	4
1 whole wheat dinner roll (1-1/2 ounces)	110
Total Calories	586

Place halibut on plate and cover with plastic wrap. Cook for two minutes in a microwave set at "high." Rotate the plate. Microwave for an additional two minutes or until fish flakes easily with fork. (Poaching or steaming are other low-calorie ways to cook white fish.)

Make sauce for the fish by combining yogurt, cocktail sauce and lemon juice. Mix well. Pour over cooked fish. Place fish back in microwave briefly to heat the sauce.

Place vegetables on top of pre-cooked rice. Heat. Make liquid Butter Buds following the instructions on the box; pour over rice and vegetables. Butter Buds can also be used on the dinner roll if desired.

Comment

People are eating more fish today — and for good reason! Fish is generally high in nutrients and low in fat and calories. One ounce of just about any kind of white fish provides five or six grams of high-quality protein, a small amount of fat and fewer than 30 calories. In contrast, an ounce of T-bone steak has 10 grams of fat and 100 calories. What's more, according to the *Tufts University Diet & Nutrition Letter,* fish protein is more easily digested than animal protein because fish has less connective tissue.

It's important, however, to select low-fat varieties of fish. In general, the darker the color of the flesh, the higher the fat and calorie content. Examples of the fattier varieties of fish include herring, mackerel, trout, catfish, sardines and salmon. The halibut in this recipe, and other white fish such as cod, sole, flounder, haddock and orange roughy, are low in fat and calories. Orange roughy is a white fish that Carol and I discovered recently; it's tender and has a delicious, mild flavor. If you see it at the market, give it a try. We think you'll like it.

Fish may also be good for your heart. Dutch researchers studied more than 850 men over a 20-year period, and found that those who ate fish had a lower incidence of heart disease. The research, reported in the *New England Journal of Medicine,* revealed that men who ate one ounce or more of fish a day were about 2-1/2 times less likely to die from heart disease than men who ate none.

Interestingly, the fish eaters consumed more cholesterol and fat than the men who ate no fish. So why didn't that contribute to heart disease? The explanation, the Dutch researchers wrote, may be a fatty acid in fish called eicosapentaenoic acid. This acid — it's found in both lean and fatty fish — appears to reduce the blood clots that clog blood vessels and threaten the heart. The researchers concluded that eating "as little as one or two fish dishes per week may be of preventive value."

Whatever its preventive effect on heart disease, white fish is good for bodybuilders and anyone else who wants to stay lean because of its high protein and low fat/calorie content. Nevertheless, I still eat fish in relatively small portions. Like other flesh food, it contains little or no fiber; overdose on it and you'll get constipated. Carol and I freeze halibut steaks cut into five-ounce servings.

Carol likes her fish plain, but most readers will probably agree with me that the tomato-yogurt sauce included here makes it better. I selected Del Monte brand seafood cocktail sauce because it contains no added fat. It does have added sweeteners and salt, however. Before an important event, you'll probably want to flavor your fish with lemon juice only.

I first heard of Butter Buds when I read Dr. Robert Haas' book,

Remember to stick with small portions of white fish and pass up the darker colored, fattier varieties. *Photo by Guy Appelman.*

70

Eat To Win (Rawson Associates, 1983). Like the fish sauce, they make this meal taste better. Butter Buds are available in supermarkets everywhere. They taste like butter, but contain no fat. An ounce of liquid Butter Buds (two tablespoons) has only 12 calories, compared to 200 calories in an equal amount of butter or margarine. Butter Buds are excellent poured over cooked vegetables and rice.

The only bad thing about them is the sodium. I don't know the exact sodium content but, judging by the taste, it's quite high. So when sodium is a concern, skip the Butter Buds.

Now to reiterate the main lesson I've been trying to impart in discussing this meal: Stick with small portions of white fish; this type of fish is best because it's leaner. Pass up the darker-colored fattier fish.

HALF CHICKEN BREAST, POTATO & VEGETABLES

	Calories
4 ounces skinned and boned chicken breast (weight cooked)	190
3 tablespoons tomato sauce, canned without sugar or fat added	15
1 large baked potato (7 ounces cooked)	185
4 ounces frozen corn, broccoli and red peppers (no salt added)	82
4 tablespoons liquid Butter Buds	24
1 sliced tomato (5 ounces)	31
Dash of pepper	—
1 whole wheat roll (1.5 ounces)	110
Total Calories	637

Place chicken breast on a plate and cover with waxed paper. Cook for about eight minutes in a microwave set at "high," or until chicken can be easily pierced with a fork.* Take chicken out of oven, remove the skin and pull the meat off the bone. Spoon tomato sauce over boned chicken breast. Microwave for an additional two minutes at medium heat, or until chicken and sauce are hot.

Bake potato and heat vegetables; use Butter Buds as a topping for both. Butter Buds can also be used on the dinner roll, if you like. Serve sliced tomato on the side with pepper.

Comment

Poultry, like fish, is low in fat and calories. Generally, chicken contains more calories than fish, however. For example, the four ounces of chicken in this recipe provides 190 calories, while the five ounces of halibut in the previous meal provides only 143 calories.

Again, as in the case with fish, the white meat of chicken has less fat and fewer calories than the dark meat. That's why chicken breast is a good choice. Also, much of the fat in chicken is in the skin. By removing the skin after cooking as suggested here, you reduce the calories substantially.

My wife and I eat chicken in small portions. We buy half chicken breasts and store them in the freezer for use one at a time. On the average, half a chicken breast weighs about four ounces. We think that's a good serving size.

Of course, many bodybuilders eat chicken in much larger portions — eight ounces or more. They consider chicken an excellent source of low-calorie protein... and it is! The problem is that by eating so much chicken to get the protein, they often end up consuming more calories than they need. Increasing the chicken in this recipe to eight ounces would add 18 grams of protein and 190 calories. More than likely, however, the extra protein would be deposited as fat. What's more, the extra meat would probably clog the digestive system. In my view, it's best not to overdo a good thing.

In their book *Supercut* (Contemporary Books, 1985), Bill Reynolds and Dr. Joyce Vedral observe that the skinned white meat of chicken has come to be known as "the most boring food imaginable" — that is, by bodybuilders who regularly make a complete meal out of white chicken meat. Needless to say, I don't recommend that. It's true that plain chicken can get monotonous. But eaten with Butter Buds, baked potato, vegetables and bread, plus the added spice of tomato sauce, chicken is anything but

The skinned, white meat of chicken is pretty boring, but spiced with tomato sauce and eaten with bread and vegetables it's a feast. *Photo by John Balik.*

boring. It's a feast to delight a gourmet bodybuilder.

You can buy tomato sauce at any supermarket, but I usually get mine at a health food store. This sauce has tomatoes, salt, onion powder, garlic powder and spices. Since it contains no sugar or fat, it adds a lot of flavor for only a few extra calories — only 15 in the three tablespoons used here. Of course, tomato sauce usually contains salt. If this is a problem, you can buy tomato sauce with no salt added. It won't taste as good, however. Normally, I let my tastebuds rule; I don't worry about the sodium in a small amount of tomato sauce — about 65 milligrams per tablespoon.

One more thing: mixed vegetables usually have fewer calories than individual vegetables. For instance, corn alone would provide approximately 25 percent more calories than the corn, broccoli and red pepper combination in this meal. That's because broccoli and red pepper have fewer calories than corn; an ounce of corn has about 24 calories compared to only nine in an ounce of broccoli. If you haven't done so already, I suggest that you check out the many vegetable combinations available in the frozen food section of your supermarket. You'll save calories and, as a bonus, you'll also get a taste treat.

* Chicken is sometimes contaminated with salmonella bacteria, and must be cooked thoroughly to ensure that this organism is destroyed. Microwave ovens often undercook in spots, so be careful. A rotating microwave tray solves this problem beautifully. I suggest that you buy one.

WHOLE WHEAT MACARONI, CHEESE & VEGETABLES

	Calories
3 ounces whole wheat macaroni (dry weight)	315
3 tablespoons (2 ounces) Ragu "no sugar added" spaghetti sauce	35
1 ounce mozzarella cheese, shredded	85
1/2 cup nonfat yogurt (calories vary by brand)	50
4 ounces frozen Italian vegetables (zucchini squash, cauliflower, carrots, Italian green beans, lima beans and slight amount of salt)	34
1 whole wheat dinner roll (1-1/2 ounces)	110
Total Calories	629

Cook macaroni according to instructions on the package. Drain. Place macaroni in a large dish. Make cheese sauce by combining spaghetti sauce, shredded cheese and nonfat yogurt; mix well. Add cheese sauce to macaroni and mix until macaroni is evenly coated. Place vegetables on top of macaroni. Place in microwave and heat until cheese is melted and all the ingredients are warm. (If you prefer, vegetables can be topped with Butter Buds and served on the side.)

Comment

Contrary to popular opinion, pasta is not fattening. The three ounces of dry pasta in this recipe expands to about 7-1/2 ounces when cooked and provides only 315 calories. That's not many calories for so much food. The same amount of T-bone steak has about 750 calories. The difference, of course, is that steak is fatty, while pasta is mainly carbohydrate with almost no fat. Pasta, like bread and potatoes, is good diet food. It fills you up and makes you feel satisfied, while giving you relatively few calories.

I use whole wheat pasta instead of the white flour, enriched variety because it has more fiber and, therefore, is chewier and more filling. Whole wheat pasta has not had the fiber, vitamins and minerals discarded in the milling process. "Enriched" pasta has some vitamins and minerals returned, but the fiber is not replaced. Nutritionist Nancy Clark says, "Pasta, made from refined white flour, is little more than fluffy white bread." Nevertheless, many people like the taste of regular pasta and white bread. That's why companies sell so much of the stuff. But although the calorie content of both types of pasta is about the same, whole wheat pasta is better for weight-conscious people because it provides more chewing satisfaction and fills you up better.

Actually, this whole meal is great for filling you up but keeping the calories down. We've already talked about the calorie advantages of mozzarella cheese, nonfat yogurt and mixed vegetables. Now let's look at the Ragu "no sugar added" spaghetti sauce, which rounds out the flavor of this meal nicely. Even though this

Be sure to try whole wheat pasta. It's chewier and more filling than the fluffy, white stuff that's usually served. *Photo by Guy Appelman.*

sauce contains fat in the form of soybean oil, it contributes only 35 calories to this recipe. That's because I use only one-third as much sauce as suggested on the label. There's no need to drown the pasta in sauce. Use just enough to provide the desired taste. You'll probably find that a little sauce goes a long way.

If you have a contest coming up, note that there's sodium in the Ragu sauce. Cheese contains salt as well, and there's a little salt in the vegetables. If it's important for you to avoid sodium entirely, skip the cheese and use sauce and vegetables without added salt.

Whatever you decide about the salt, be sure to try whole wheat pasta. It's delicious. You'll find it at your health food store. Two brands that I like are Westbrae and De Boles.

THE RIPPED SLOPPY JOE

	Calories
1/2 cup pinto beans with chili sauce (canned, no sugar or fat added)	140
2 ounces lean ground beef (weight raw)	100
4 ounces frozen okra and tomatoes	31
1/2 cup nonfat yogurt (calories vary by brand)	50
3 tablespoons green chile sauce (no sugar or fat added)	24
3 slices whole wheat bread, toasted	270
Total Calories	615

Cook ground beef and pour off the fat that appears in the skillet. Break meat into small pieces. Combine beef, beans, yogurt, vegetables and sauce; mix well. Heat. Serve over bread.

Comment

I included this recipe just for fun. There's nothing much more to say about it. I've commented on almost all the ingredients in connection with other recipes.

Try the Ripped Sloppy Joe when you feel like a spicy change of pace.

DINING OUT

If you only eat out occasionally, go ahead and order whatever appeals to you. Nobody ever got fat on one meal. It's what you eat day after day that determines whether you're fat or lean. If you eat out regularly, however, it's important to know how to order wisely. You must be able to search out the non-fattening items on the menu. I'll give you some suggestions that should help.

First, avoid fast-food restaurants. Fast foods typically lack fiber and are high in fat, calories and sodium. You can blow your calorie allowance in a flash. For example, a McDonald's Big Mac has 561 calories, 53 percent of which come from fat. Add fries and a Coke and you're over 900 calories! Your waistline will show it if you frequent the burger, chicken, pizza, taco and fish places. They have little to offer a weight-conscious person.

I can count on the fingers of one hand the times I've eaten fast food in the last few years. If you've lost count, it's probably time for you to look around for other places to eat. If there's simply nothing else available, try brown bagging it. A peanut butter lunch (like mine) is easy to take with you anytime.

Nancy Clark, in her book *The Athlete's Kitchen* (Bantam Books, 1983), observes that the most popular restaurants are those that serve the largest portions. Don't tempt yourself by going to those places — if you're at all like me, you'll probably end up eating until you're about to burst. And, of course, it goes without saying that you should skip the all-you-can-eat restaurants; they're dangerous.

Do you fly frequently? When you travel by plane, you may feel like you're trapped in the air with fattening foods. Well, there's a number of things you can do to protect yourself. First, turn down the honey-roasted nuts the attendants hand out as soon as you're airborne. As I've already said, nuts are mostly fat and packed with calories. I hand mine back to the attendant, smile and say, "Here, I'm afraid I might eat these."

Don't munch on nuts just to pass the time. Why not read the latest *Muscle & Fitness* or some other magazine instead. The time will go by quicker and you won't gain an ounce.

Actually, airline food generally isn't bad. I usually eat most of what's served. If meat is the main course, however, I concentrate on the side dishes and leave most of the meat. I also pass up the dessert. When I've eaten what I want, I give the tray back to the attendant as soon as possible. Again, I don't want to tempt myself.

If you don't think you can resist the high-calorie portion of an in-flight meal (it does take some willpower), call ahead for one of the low-calorie meals most airlines offer. You might want to try a vegetarian plate or a big salad. If you're on the way to a contest, ask for a low-sodium meal. And if you want to be extra careful, bring your own food. It's easy to stick a hard-boiled egg, a baked potato and some fruit in your carry-on bag.

When eating in restaurants (remember, we warned you about the fast-food and all-you-can-eat places), the key is to order plain foods so you can tell exactly what you're getting. Stick with food served the way Mother Nature made it — unprocessed, with nothing removed and nothing added. Follow the same rules you do at home. Select foods that have all the fiber left in, and no sugar or fat added.

Here are some general guidelines to follow:

• Specify that your food be cooked without oil or butter. Fried or breaded food is always higher in calories. That's true of gravy and sauces as well; they're usually loaded with salt and fat.

• If you want meat, choose fish and chicken over beef or pork. Remember, white fish and the white meat of chicken is lower in calories. I talked about white fish earlier. Some other good bets are lobster tails, crab legs and scallops; have them steamed, boiled or broiled without butter. Again, watch out for the sauce.

• Green and starchy vegetables are a good selection, if you can get them without butter or sauce. *Eat To Win* author Robert Haas suggests taking along Butter Buds to sprinkle on vegetables in place of the butter or sauce served in the restaurant. That's a good idea.

• Fresh fruit is a good choice for dessert. Coffee with milk and an artificial sweetener is another good way to satisfy your sweet tooth.

Often when you're eating out you have to make spur-of-the-moment nutritional decisions, often with a waiter standing over you. We can't anticipate every question that might arise, but here are suggestions for dealing with some of the more common ones:

Should you eat the hot rolls the waiter brings to keep you busy until your order comes? Sure. If you're really hungry, go ahead and have a roll or two, but leave the butter off. Remember, bread is good diet food. It'll take the edge off your appetite, and you'll have more control when the main course arrives.

What dressing should you have on your salad? Vinegar and oil is a good choice; order them in separate containers so you can decide how much oil goes on your salad. If you'd prefer another dressing, have it served on the side also, so you can decide how much to put on the salad.

What if there's a salad bar? By all means, take advantage of it. Salad bars are great for dieters, but only if they're used right. Stick with fresh, unadorned salad fixings such as lettuce, cabbage, tomato, cauliflower, broccoli, cucumbers, bell peppers and sprouts. Garbanzo beans (chickpeas) are another good choice, but you should realize that they're higher in fat and calories than other beans — five grams of fat and 340 calories to the cup.

Leave the mixtures alone. There's nothing low-calorie about potato salad, macaroni salad, chicken salad, etc. They all have added calories in the form of sugar, oil or mayonnaise. Fresh fruit is a good selection, but fruit salad probably isn't low in calories. Skip it as well. When eating from a salad bar follow this rule: Select the items that look like they came straight from the garden or the orchard, and pass up the rest.

What kind of potato should you order? I always order a plain baked potato — no butter, no sour cream. As I'm sure you know, hash browns and French fries are loaded with fat. The same is usually true of mashed potatoes. I think you'll find that baked potato is good eaten plain or moistened with a little vinegar. Still, if you must have butter with your potato, use Butter Buds. Just stick a packet in your pocket and use it any time you want the taste, but not the calories, of butter.

What if you can't find an acceptable main course on the menu? Order eggs. They're available in most restaurants. Add toast, sliced tomatoes, a baked potato, coffee, and you're in business. Be careful how the eggs are cooked, however. Scrambled eggs and

80

My number one rule when eating out is: keep it simple. *Photo by Guy Appelman.*

omelets should be avoided because they're usually cooked with lots of grease. Poached eggs are best. Two poached eggs provide only 164 calories, but those same two eggs scrambled or in an omelet give you 222 calories.

Again, the most important suggestion I can give you about eating out: Keep it simple. Plain food is best; you can tell whether it has sugar or fat added. Fancy dishes are almost always fattening.

SNACKS

Snacks are important for appetite control. I eat a mid-afternoon and bedtime snack almost every day. Eating between meals keeps me from overeating. Sounds strange, doesn't it? But it's true.

Each workday morning, Carol and I prepare snacks to take to the office. It's usually something simple like baked potatoes. I have nonfat yogurt with mine; she likes mozzarella cheese with hers. You see, we agree with nutritionist Nancy Clark, author of *The Athlete's Kitchen* (Bantam Books, 1983), that planned snacking is better than the "starve and stuff" routine.

When I'm at the office, I usually don't feel hungry until lunch. But the afternoon is a different story. By mid-afternoon, I'm dragging a little and need a snack. That's when I have the baked potato and yogurt at my desk. This perks me up until quitting time. More important, it keeps me from being ravenously hungry when I get home. If I'm only moderately hungry at the dinner table, it's easier to stop eating when I'm comfortably full. But if I'm starving when I sit down to dinner, as I would be without my snack, I'm more likely to stuff myself.

The snack I have about an hour before going to bed controls my appetite in a similar fashion. First, it keeps me from going to bed hungry, then getting up during the night to raid the refrigerator. Also, since I can look forward to a substantial bedtime snack, it helps me avoid snacking haphazardly throughout the evening. My planned late-night snack gives me the calories I need — and no more! That leaves me feeling satisfied until breakfast.

Planned eating between meals is a good idea, but don't make the mistake of snacking on sugary sweets. The donut or candy bar that many people eat for a pick-me-up may give them a temporary energy boost, but usually winds up making them more tired. That's because the sugar in these popular snacks triggers the pancreas to secrete extra insulin. This insulin can pull the blood sugar level way down. The result is usually less energy, not more.

The answer is to snack on fruit, vegetables, whole grains and dairy products. The sugar from these foods is absorbed slowly into the bloodstream, so you don't get a sudden release of insulin. As a consequence, these foods give you lasting energy and satisfy your

Planned snacking will help you become lean and stay that way. *Photo by Guy Appelman.*

appetite longer.

Here are some of my favorite snacks taken from my training diaries. They're all tasty and filling, but the really good news is that none of them exceed 250 calories.

- Two-thirds cup brown rice, one ounce raisins and one-half cup skimmed milk.
- One-half cup nonfat yogurt* (with one-half ounce Post Grape-Nuts Nuggets sprinkled on top), one cup fresh strawberries and one slice whole grain bread.
- One large baked potato and one cup nonfat yogurt.*
- Fruit (apple, banana or pear), one slice whole grain bread and one-half cup skimmed milk.
- One cup nonfat yogurt* and three rice cakes topped with an ounce of fruit spread.
- One cup winter squash (baked) and one cup nonfat yogurt.*
- Two shredded wheat biscuits topped with two-thirds cup skimmed milk and Equal sweetener (optional).
- One-half cantaloupe and one cup low-fat (1%) cottage cheese.
- Two sliced tomatoes topped with one cup nonfat yogurt* and an ounce of raisins.
- One baked sweet potato (5 ounces) and two-thirds cup skimmed milk.
- One large carrot, one cup nonfat yogurt* and one ounce dried apricots.
- One ear of corn and one cup nonfat yogurt.*
- Two slices whole-grain raisin bread and one-half cup nonfat yogurt.*
- One banana, two-thirds cup skimmed milk and three crispy, squared rice cakes.
- Two-thirds ounce mozzarella cheese, one slice whole wheat bread and an apple.
- Two slices whole wheat bread topped with the following — one-half cup nonfat yogurt* and one teaspoon apple butter (no sugar added), mixed together.

Remember, don't starve and stuff. Snack!

* I use Alta-Dena nonfat yogurt (calorie content: 100 per cup). If the brand you use has more calories, reduce the amount accordingly.

Photo by Guy Appelman.

PART TWO

The
Routines

PART TWO: The Routines

EXERCISE: THE MOST IMPORTANT FACTOR IN GETTING RIPPED

Diet is actually the second most important factor in getting ripped. Exercise is the first. As a practical matter, it's almost impossible to control your body fat level without regular exercise. That's because leanness depends, to a large extent, on activity. The more active you are, the leaner you're likely to be. That seems to be nature's way. Your body tends to mirror your lifestyle.

Think about it. Can you conceive of ancient man as anything but lean? I can't. Obesity would have no place in a world where you had to run down your dinner and move from region to region with the seasons, like a migrating bird, to survive.

In modern times, animals show the close relationship between exercise and leanness. Wild animals are both active and lean. Only in captivity do they get fat.

Of course, athletes (especially endurance athletes) carry very little body fat even though they often eat a tremendous amount of food, including the calorie-dense variety. These same athletes, however, typically put on body fat if they stop training. The body seems to sense that an active person (or animal) needs to be lean and, conversely, that a sedentary person does not.

Science has attempted to explain this through a concept called the body fat setpoint, which I discuss in *The Lean Advantage*. Many scientists believe that each of us has a variable, internal mechanism that dictates how much fat we carry. This internal thermostat maintains a "set" amount of fat on the body. It increases our appetite when we fall below the setpoint and decreases it when we go above it. It also speeds up the body's metabolism to "waste" excess calories if we overeat and slows the metabolism down to "conserve" energy when we don't eat enough.

Activity is the single most important factor in determining whether our body fat setpoint is high or low. Active people, i.e., people who exercise, have a lower fat setpoint than those who are sedentary, and they usually have no trouble maintaining a low body fat level. Inactive people have a higher fat setpoint, which makes it difficult for them to become lean.

It's well known that aerobic exercise — walking, jogging, swimming, biking and other rhythmic activities that are continued for a long period of time — lowers the body fat setpoint. Aerobic exercise burns extra calories, but it does more than burn calories while you exercise. It also speeds up your metabolism so you burn more calories long after you finish exercising! As I explain in *Ripped 2,* aerobic exercise also increases the fat-burning enzymes in your muscles, allowing you to convert fat to energy more efficiently. Biopsies have shown that endurance athletes have a greater number of fat-burning enzymes than non-athletes.

People who are out of shape, and have few fat-burning enzymes, burn the sugar in their blood and muscle tissue (rather than fat) for fuel. In other words, the energy in their fat cells stays put. Aerobically fit people, on the other hand, burn fat readily. That makes it easier for them to keep the fat off.

The role of weight training in staying lean isn't as well known or acknowledged. Many authors mistakenly downplay the effectiveness of weight training in body fat control. They say, correctly, that weight training doesn't produce a high level of aerobic fitness and isn't carried on long enough to burn a substantial number of calories. They, however, ignore an important fact: Nothing else builds and maintains muscle tissue as well as weight training. And, of course, the amount of muscle you have is critical to body fat regulation, because 90 percent of the calories burned in your body are burned by the muscles.

Therefore, well-muscled bodybuilders have a big advantage over those who don't lift weights. Their added muscle mass burns extra calories 24 hours a day, even during sleep. A champion bodybuilder has proportionately more calorie-burning muscle tissue than a champion marathoner. But that's not the end of it. A champion bodybuilder who's also aerobically fit has more fat-burning capacity *than just about anybody.* He or she truly has the lean advantage.

Exercise is the key to body fat control. A fit and well-muscled bodybuilder has more fat-burning capacity than just about anybody. *Photo by Bill Reynolds.*

Finally, diet alone has a notoriously poor record in body fat control. Only a miniscule percentage of people who lose weight by dieting keep it off. Actually, severe dieting may be a major factor in obesity, because it triggers the body's starvation defenses; it slows the metabolism, and research has shown that it also increases the enzymes responsible for depositing fat on the body. The level of fat-depositing enzymes is dramatically higher in people who have lost weight through severe calorie restriction. That's one reason why these people typically gain back all the fat they lost — and more! Another reason, of course, is that dieting makes them hungry.

The bottom line, therefore, is that exercise is the key to body fat control. It burns calories but, more importantly, it lowers the body fat setpoint and increases fat-burning capacity. Diet alone doesn't work. Diet plus aerobic exercise is more effective. The best combination of all, however, is a balanced diet of natural foods, aerobic exercise and weight training. This three-pronged approach will make you lean for life.

ABOUT THE ROUTINES

"The key — the absolute key — to bodybuilding success is *variation*." That's what Fred Hatfield, exercise physiologist, editor-in-chief of *Sports Fitness* magazine and 1983 world power-lifting champion, wrote about training in *Bodybuilding: A Scientific Approach* (Contemporary Books, 1984). I may favor a uniform eating plan (for reasons already explained) so far as nutrition is concerned, but when it comes to actual training, I believe Fred is dead-on correct about the importance of variety. In fact, my own research and experience support his conclusion. That's why the cornerstone of the Ripped training routines is variety, planned variety.

Auburn University's Dr. Mike Stone, perhaps the preeminent strength training researcher in the country, says that staleness and lack of progress is often the result of a "monotonous, unvarying training routine" (bodybuilders, take note!). The body grows stronger from a specific workout or set of exercises, but after a time the sheer monotony tends to tire the body so it can't respond anymore.

This is consistent with the well-known "General Adaptation Syndrome" formulated by Dr. Hans Selye in the early 1930s. According to Selye's theory, an athlete goes through three distinct phases of adaptation during training. The first phase, the "alarm stage," is characterized by a temporary drop in performance due to stiffness and muscle soreness. During the second stage, called the "resistance stage," the body adapts to the stress of training and becomes stronger. But if training is continued too long, then "exhaustion," the third stage, is reached. During the third stage desirable adaptation is no longer possible.

Dr. Stone and his co-author Harold S. O'Bryant, Ph.D., explain in the preliminary edition of *Weight Training: A Scientific Approach* (Burgess Publishing Company, Minneapolis, Minn., 1984) that monotonous routines speed the onset of the exhaustion stage. Stone and O'Bryant add that study after research study, starting with the work of Soviet sports scientist Dmitri Matveyev in the early 1960s, has shown that the best gains in strength and muscle mass come when variation is introduced into the training routine.

Matveyev developed a training model which he called "Periodization." It forms the basis for most modern-day variable routines. In his system, training is done in cycles of gradually increasing intensity, followed by periods of easier training. In each cycle, training intensity is increased by beginning with light weights and high repetitions and gradually progressing, in distinct periods, to heavy weights and low repetitions.

Since Matveyev originated this concept, at least 17 research projects — the subjects have included untrained men and women, football teams, a woman's softball team, advanced weight trainers, Olympic lifters and various other athletes — have proven the effectiveness of periodization compared to the traditional three-sets-of-10 approach. The studies monitored a number of different variables, but bodybuilders will be especially interested to know that periodization produced greater gains in lean body mass and greater decreases in body fat. Let's take a look at Matveyev's

Planned variety is the key to bodybuilding success. *Photo by Guy Appelman.*

model as it's usually applied, and then analyze how it can best be applied to bodybuilding.

Periodization usually involves three training phases: high repetition-light weight (the hypertrophy phase); medium repetition-medium weight (the basic strength phase); and low repetition-heavy weight (the power phase). This is usually followed by an active rest period in which the athlete does only a few repetitions with very light weights. Each of the training phases has a specific purpose. Taken together, they're designed to bring the athlete to a competitive peak.

The hypertrophy (muscle increase) phase prepares the athlete physiologically to lift heavier weights later in the cycle. Three or more sets of eight to 12 repetitions are used in each exercise. This increases lean muscle mass and builds short-term muscular endurance. According to Dr. Stone, these adaptations increase the potential of the athlete to gain strength and power.

In the basic strength phase, the weights are increased and the repetitions are decreased to the four to six range. With the base (in terms of increased muscle size and endurance) provided by the hypertrophy phase, strength increases sharply during this second phase. The strength gained here prepares the athlete to lift even heavier weights in the power phase. Unfortunately, Dr. Stone reports that the lower volume of work in the last two phases of the cycle (i.e., the strength and power phases) can result in a slight increase in body fat and a slight decrease in muscle mass. This negative effect is usually countered by adding a concluding set, or a backoff set, of 10 repetitions to each exercise in the workout.

Strength and power are brought to a peak in the third phase through a combination of very heavy weights and low repetitions. For example, the athlete might do three to five sets of two or three repetitions with heavy weights. With such low repetitions the body is less fatigued, and the athlete can concentrate on doing fast, explosive repetitions. The heavy weights and emphasis on speed during this phase condition the central nervous system to perform at peak efficiency, sending the strongest possible message to the muscles to contract maximally. No wonder the highest levels of strength and power are achieved during this phase.

94

Of course, when the athlete starts the whole cycle over again, the explosive power developed here will allow heavier weights to be used and more muscle mass to be added during the next hypertrophy phase. That's because, Dr. Stone explains, the muscular endurance required in the first phase largely depends on the maximum strength level of the muscles being used. Simply put, muscles that are conditioned to lift more weight for two or three repetitions can also lift more weight for 10 or 12 repetitions. In other words, you begin the next cycle of training poised to achieve a higher peak. Each succeeding training cycle leaves you bigger and stronger than the one before.

However, the active rest period is also critical to the overall strength and muscle-building process. After you've spent several months achieving a peak, your mental and physical batteries need time to recharge. So set a week or two aside to toy with very light weights, ride your bike or do something else you enjoy. Dr. Stone says the rest period at the end of the training cycle is very important: "It reduces the possibility of overtraining during the next cycle."

Before getting into the details of periodization for bodybuilders, let me elaborate on why this system works so well. Periodization is the best way to train because its cycle of increasing intensity and decreasing volume allows the body to gradually adapt to the stress of weight training. That's the physiological reason why it's the best way to train, but there are psychological benefits as well. And that brings us back to... variety!

Prof. Terry Todd and his researcher wife, Jan, are on the faculty at the University of Texas (Austin). Former world-class power-lifters, they talk about the psychological benefits of periodization in their book, *Lift Your Way to Youthful Fitness* (Little, Brown & Company, 1985): "Boredom kills more fitness programs than any other villain.... People get tired of doing the same thing all the time, whether it's working on an assembly line or running laps around a small indoor track. The advantage of periodization is that no two workouts are ever the same. Every day you'll either vary the exercises, the poundages, or the number of repetitions so that you have different things to think about, different goals."

The Todds add a second and possibly even more important

Because of the variety it offers, periodization is more interesting than any other method of weight training. *Photo by Bill Reynolds.*

THE RIPPED CYCLE SYSTEM

Phase	Duration	Repetitions	Sets	Frequency	Intensity	Performance
Endurance	4 weeks	20 (15-25)	1 or 2 (after warm-up)	3-4 days a week	Hard/easy	Slow, continuous reps
Strength & Endurance	4 weeks	12 (10-15)	1 or 2 (after warm-up)	3-4 days a week	Hard/easy	Moderate speed, with pause between reps
Strength	4 weeks	8 (6-10)	1 or 2 (after warm-up)	3-4 days a week	Hard/easy	Fast (but controlled), with pause between reps
Recovery	1 or 2 weeks	Your choice	1	2 days a week	Very easy	Your choice

psychological benefit: "Periodization has a built-in reward system. By increasing your training poundages gradually, you condition yourself to succeed and your self-confidence will grow."

It's simple, really. Because of the variety it offers, periodization is more interesting than any other method of weight training. What's more, it utilizes that greatest of all motivators, success, to keep you training and improving. Success breeds success.

Now let's examine the form of periodization I use and recommend for bodybuilders. Look at the chart outlining The Ripped Cycle System. You'll notice I recommend higher repetitions than the number used in the standard periodization program. That's because bodybuilders are interested in maximum size, not maximum strength.

Research done by L.E. Morehouse and A.T. Miller in 1978 suggests that eight to 20 repetitions are best for building size. That's the range most bodybuilders use. Moreover, as I mentioned earlier when I talked about the strength and power phases of a periodization program, low repetitions (three to five) may actually cause a *loss* of muscle size. Another problem is that low repetitions with very heavy weights increase the potential for injury to the muscles and joints. The one or two minor, but chronic, injuries I have stem from my Olympic lifting days when I did heavy singles and rarely went over five reps. In short, low reps simply have no place in a bodybuilder's program.

Fred Hatfield, who squatted with a stupendous 1,008 pounds at the 1986 Budweiser World Record Breakers contest in Hawaii, agrees that low reps have little, if anything, to offer a bodybuilder. He adds this telling comment: "Even powerlifters are learning that maximum singles in training do not help them get stronger over the long term. Most powerlifters have retreated, so to speak, to the five-eight-reps-per-set method for strength training, leaving the singles for the contest."

This reinforces what I say in *Ripped 2*: "If you perform less than six repetitions you probably won't exhaust a high percentage of muscle fibers. Low repetitions may be good for testing strength, but they're not the best way to build muscle size and strength."

Why do eight to 20 repetitions build muscle size best? Actually, there's more involved than simply doing that many reps. It all comes back to the need for variety that I spotlighted at the beginning of this section. It takes high reps, low reps, fast reps, slow reps, continuous-tension reps, rest-pause reps — the entire combination — to force a muscle to grow to maximum size.

A muscle cell has a number of different parts, all of which contribute to the overall size of the cell. As Fred Hatfield explains in *Bodybuilding: A Scientific Approach*, "Each component has a specific function to perform, and by overloading that function you will force that component to develop in size or quantity — this is the way our body 'protects' itself from destructive stress. By varying the stress you will ensure that maximum growth and development is achieved."

To a bodybuilder, the two most important components of a muscle cell are the myofibrils and the mitochondria. Focus your training on these two parts and the other components will take care of themselves.

The myofibrils are the contractile or strength component of the muscle cells, and the mitochondria are the endurance component. Generally speaking, the size of the myofibrils is proportional to the contractile strength of the muscle and the size of the mitochondria is proportional to the endurance capacity.

Six to 10 fast (explosive) repetitions with maximum poundage are best for increasing the size of the myofibrils, while 15 to 25 slow, controlled reps increase both the size and number of the mitochondria. Reps in the mid range (10-15), performed with moderate speed, stress both the strength and endurance components of the muscle. Therefore, you can see that all three repetition ranges and speeds of movement are necessary to develop a muscle to its maximum size.

Admittedly, this is a simplistic way to think of the myofibrils and mitochondria; the function and structure of the components of a muscle cell are actually quite complex. Nevertheless, I find that thinking about it this clear-cut way gives my training a sharper focus. It allows me to visualize what's going on in my muscles. Whereas, if I let myself get bogged down in the physiological minutiae, it's easy to become confused.

With a clear picture in your mind of what you're trying to accomplish, your training concentration is better. When you understand the task at hand clearly and concisely, you can do a better job... of bodybuilding or anything else, for that matter. So don't let yourself get so mired in the details that you can't see the forest for the trees.

Nevertheless, if you're still curious and want more details on the structure and function of muscle cells, I recommend Dr. Hatfield's book, *Bodybuilding: A Scientific Approach* (it's available from Ripped Enterprises). You might also go to the library and check out a textbook entitled *Exercise Physiology* by William D. McCardle, Frank I. Katch and Victor L. Katch (Lea & Febiger, 1986). This book can be found in most university libraries.

Before we leave the myofibrils and mitochondria, there's one more tip I'd like to give you. When you feel a burn or pump in your muscles, that means the mitochondria are getting a good workout. The mitochondria are responsible for processing oxygen and also producing a chemical called ATP, which is the immediate source of energy for muscle contraction. In fact, the mitochondria are often called the "powerhouse" of the cell, because they're the structures in which food energy, or ATP, for muscle contraction is produced. Without ATP, a muscle cannot contract.

Significantly, the breakdown of ATP produces lactic acid and causes the pumped feeling in the muscles that all bodybuilders know. When you do high reps, the lactic acid accumulation, or pump, eventually makes further repetitions impossible. The number of reps you can do before lactic acid buildup shuts down the muscle is largely determined by the capacity of the mitochondria to utilize oxygen. That's because oxygen allows lactic acid to be broken down to produce energy for further contractions. On the other hand, when you use a heavier weight that only permits six to 10 reps, there isn't sufficient pump to terminate the set, so the contractile strength of the myofibrils is the limiting factor.

Again, high reps place primary stress on the mitochondrial component, and reps in the six to 10 range overload the contractile fibers, the myofibrils. When you want to work the mitochondria, do slow, continuous reps and go for the burn. To work myofibrils, lift faster and pause briefly between reps to let the pump subside. When you follow the latter approach, lactic acid doesn't interfere and the muscle can contract to its limit. Lifting faster is important because it activates more contractile fibers, especially the fast-twitch fibers which, as I explain in *The Lean Advantage,* increase in size (hypertrophy) more than do the slower contracting fibers. You should never throw

100

It takes high reps, low reps, slow reps, fast reps, continuous tension reps, rest-pause reps—all of them to develop maximum muscle size. *Photo by Bill Reynolds.*

or jerk the weight, however (more about that when we get to the actual routines).

Now look again at the chart of the Ripped Cycle System (page 97). Note that, in addition to high, medium and low repetitions, the system includes different exercise performance modes: slow, continuous reps during the endurance phase; moderate-speed reps with a pause during the strength and endurance phase; and fast reps with a pause during the strength phase. Since you've read the explanation of how to stimulate the mitochondria and the myofibrils, you can now see why this variation is necessary to develop all components of the muscle cell. In addition, there are several more important points we should consider before examining the system phase by phase.

Ripped 2 carries an extensive discussion of the hard-day, easy-day training concept, including the details of my own conversion to that principle. Therefore, I won't dwell on it here, except to reiterate that it's best not to train a body part hard more than once a week. The Todds emphasize this point in their book: "In the research work done on periodization, and this is crucial, it was found that the greatest strength increases occurred when a particular group of muscles was stressed really vigorously — maximally — only once a week.... This allows the body adequate rest, and you'll progress much faster than if you try to go heavy at each workout."

This does not mean, however, that an exercise should not be repeated during the week at lesser intensity. Research has shown that best progress is made when a muscle is worked a second time, but less intensely, during the week. As I explain in *Ripped 2,* the lighter workout maintains strength without delaying recovery.

The training routines in *Ripped 2* include some workouts that are as light as 70 percent effort (in other words, 70 percent of the poundage used in your heavy workout). Jan and Terry Todd, however, suggest that dropping to 85 percent intensity is sufficient to allow recovery to take place. Recently I've been using 85 percent on light days, and it seems to work well. So I decided not to include 70 percent workouts in this book. One 100 percent (heavy) and one 85 percent (light) workout each week seems to do the job. It's simpler, as well. Nevertheless, if you're not recovering adequately, you should follow the advice in *Ripped 2* and include a 70 percent day occasionally.

Actually, powerlifters and Olympic lifters often go as low as 60 percent. In other words, if their maximum poundage is 400 pounds, on a 60 percent day they do no more than 240. That's necessary because the heavy single attempt lifts they do require a great expenditure of nervous energy, exhausting the central nervous system. That's not true for bodybuilders who use lighter weights and do six or more repetitions. So as far as bodybuilding is concerned, the Todds are probably correct: backing off to 85 percent on light days is sufficient. You'll see exactly how this works when we go through the whole training cycle.

I'm sure you've also noticed that the chart calls for only one or two sets of each exercise after warm-up. That's a departure from the traditional three to five sets, or more, per exercise usually recommended. The difference is partly semantics, because often when people refer to sets, they include warm-up sets. When I say one or two sets, I mean "work" sets, i.e., warm-up sets are not counted. Still, I probably recommend fewer sets than most.

Personally, I don't like doing the same exercise over and over. I prefer to go on to another exercise for the same body part. By performing only one or two hard sets, I concentrate better and put more intensity into each exercise. Training is more interesting that way, too, and that's important. Remember what the Todds said about boredom: "[It] kills more fitness programs than any other villain."

You be the judge. All I ask is that you try my method. If you concentrate and put out maximum effort, I think you'll find that one or two hard sets of each exercise after warm-up provides plenty of stimulation. This is especially true when you're doing high reps. After a set or two of 20 slow, continuous reps, your muscles will not only burn, they'll be on fire! You'll be damned glad to move on to the next exercise. However, don't take my word for it. Try it. You'll see what I mean.

But let's back away for a moment to look at the big picture — the essence of what you're trying to accomplish with your training. Actually, the core concept is summed up in *Ripped 2,* in the section titled "Coaxing Long-Term Gains." In that section, we said that long-term gains must be coaxed, not forced. The best results come not from constant, unrelenting effort, but from a varied system of planned, gradual progression. You push for a while, back off, and then push again, each time peaking a little higher than before.

That's what periodization is about, gradually coaxing — not forcing — the body to get bigger and stronger. As Jan and Terry Todd have suggested, the *sine qua non* of periodization is success, not failure.

Indeed, training to failure is not part of the periodization system. Rather than concentrate on getting every last repetition in every workout, you focus on progression. After all, the essence of successful bodybuilding is progression, lifting heavier and heavier weights. By gradually increasing your training poundages, you condition yourself to success, not failure. As a result, you progress further. By not squeezing yourself dry every workout, you end up lifting more in the long run and, of course, develop bigger and stronger muscles.

You start each phase with poundages you can handle in perfect form for the desired number of repetitions. Then you gradually increase the intensity until you reach new personal highs for that phase. At the end of the phase, you really have to get cranked up — use maximum effort — to complete your heavy sets. At that point, it would be extremely difficult to increase your poundages. That's when you move on to the next phase, starting again with poundages you can handle comfortably, in perfect form, for the required number of reps. In other words, you just about — but not quite — come to a sticking point; then you switch to a new repetition range and performance mode... and your progress takes off again! It's beautiful! The planned variation in the system keeps you gaining workout after workout.

Again, failure is not part of the system. In fact, you should do your best not to miss a single rep. Jan and Terry Todd hammer this point home in *Lift Your Way to Youthful Fitness*: "You can train yourself to fail just as you can train yourself to succeed. Choosing weights that are too heavy is not only dangerous but it teaches the central nervous system to give way rather than fight through. It conditions you to fail, making subsequent failure easier."

So as we said in *Ripped 2,* you make it a point to lift a little more or do another repetition or two every workout, increasing the

104

With periodization one success leads to another. It's beautiful. *Photo by John Balik.*

105

weight continuously, but not enough to stall your progress. By stopping just short of your limit, and gradually increasing your poundages, you build confidence for the next workout. By always saving a little for next time, you maintain a positive attitude. You know you can lift more, and that's exactly what you do, week after week. One success leads to another. I'll repeat myself: it's a beautiful system!

A word of advice to beginners and those who are getting back into weight training after a long layoff: Please read the "Advice for Beginners" section in *Ripped 2*, page 109. I recommend that you follow the beginner's routine included there for at least a month or two before tackling the periodization routines in this book. A beginner should start with light weights and take the time conditioning his or her body to weight training.*

In addition, if you're over 40 or have any health problems, by all means consult your physician before starting any kind of weight-training program. After you've passed muster with your doctor and learned how your body responds to weight training by following the beginner's program, you'll be ready to move on to the first periodization routine in this book.

One more bit of advice to beginners and people resuming training after a long layoff: Be sure to ease your body *gradually* into the routines in the next section, or into any other training program, for that matter. You've got time, so take time.

* Beginners would also benefit greatly from reading Jan and Terry Todd's book, *Lift Your Way to Youthful Fitness*, to which I've referred several times in this section. (It's out of print, but you can probably find a copy at the library.) Their book includes the most painstaking and thorough advice for beginners to be found anywhere. I highly recommend it to people who believe they could benefit from reading a comprehensive guide to weight training written by two real experts on the subject.

A CYCLE RUN-THROUGH

To clarify how the Ripped Cycle System actually works, let's go through all the phases. For simplicity's sake, I'll focus on only one exercise, the Squat.

We'll assume we're dealing with a male lifter whose maximum for 20 reps in the Squat is 200 pounds, and that he always does a brief general warm-up before starting any weight workout — nothing fancy, just enough to get the blood flowing and warm up the joints. Ten reps or so of each of the following movements would be fine: Curl and extend the arms (rotate palms, up at top and down on extension) to warm up the elbows; shrug the shoulders for the traps and upper back; swing the arms to the front and then to the back (like swimming) for the shoulders; lift your knees alternately (like climbing bleachers) to loosen the hips; bend down and touch the toes (with bent knees) to warm up the lower back and hamstrings; and, finally, do some free Squats for the knees.

I do this little routine at the start of all training sessions; I recommend that you do the same or something similar. It prepares the body for exercise. It also helps you get in the mood to lift.

As you'll see, I also recommend a specific warm-up on all exercises — unless the body part is already warm from a previous exercise.

In addition, at the end of each workout I either repeat my general warm-up routine or take a short, 20-minute walk. This brings my circulation back to normal. It also helps my muscles get rid of waste products, which speeds recovery and reduces muscle stiffness.

(For more information on proper warm-up and cool-down, read the following sections in *The Lean Advantage*: "Too Much Warm-up," p. 88, "Recovery Training," p. 96, and "Stationary Biking for Bodybuilders," p. 109.)

Okay, let's get started.

THE ENDURANCE PHASE

Week One

    Monday — Heavy (100% for this week)

        Squats: 115 x 8 (warm-up)

                    155 x 6 (warm-up)

                    180 x 20 (work set)

Yes, I know, this lifter can do 20 reps with 200 pounds. But, remember, we're starting with a weight that can be done in perfect

I do a brief general warm-up without weights before every training session. *Photo by Guy Appelman.*

style. Not a light weight, mind you, but a poundage that can be handled with energy to spare. This allows you to build up momentum at the start of the phase. Be patient; it'll get tough soon enough.

Thursday — Light (85%)
    Squats: 100 x 8 (warm-up)
                   130 x 6 (warm-up)
                   155 x 20 (work set)

Note that all poundages are dropped back to 85 percent, including the warm-up sets. As a rule of thumb, you can use about 65 percent of the target weight (155 here) for the first warm-up set and 85 percent for the second. You'll see that the warm-up is a little different when we get to the heavier weights in later phases. That's because you need more warm-up sets when you use heavier weights and lower reps.

You may be wondering how much rest time to take between sets. There's no rule on this, no set time. The best guideline I can give you is: Don't rush, but don't let your muscles get cold, either. Simply rest long enough to catch your breath and prepare mentally for the next set. It stands to reason, of course, that you'll need more rest on an exhausting exercise like the Squat than on an exercise such as the Curl, which causes little overall body fatigue. Again, take the rest you need, but don't sit around and lose your training drive; don't break the rhythm of the work out.

Week Two
    Monday — Heavy (100%)
        Squats: 125 x 8 (warm-up)
                      160 x 6 (warm-up)
                      190 x 20 (work set)

The weight is still quite manageable, but we're closing in on our imaginary lifter's 20-rep maximum, i.e., 200 pounds.

Take the rest you need between sets, but don't sit around and break the rhythm of the workout. *Photo by Guy Appelman.*

Thursday — Light (85%)
Squats: 105 x 8 (warm-up)
                135 x 6 (warm-up)
                160 x 20 (work-set)

This is a light day, but the workout is not a piece of cake by any means. It's enough to tax you, but not leave you drained.

Week Three
Monday — Heavy (100%)
Squats: 130 x 8 (warm-up)
                170 x 6 (warm-up)
                200 x 20 (work-set)

Our lifter equals his personal best here. It felt like a couple more reps were possible, but we saved them for the final week of the endurance phase.

Thursday — Light (85%)
Squats: 110 x 8 (warm-up)
                145 x 6 (warm-up)
                170 x 20 (work-set)

Week Four
Monday — Heavy (100%)
Squats: 135 x 8 (warm-up)
                180 x 6 (warm-up)
                210 x 22 (work-set) — personal record!

Thursday — Light (85%)
Squats: 115 x 8 (warm-up)
                155 x 6 (warm-up)
                180 x 20 (work-set)

This is the last week of the phase, so our lifter "maxed out" on the heavy day and did more than the required number of reps in the work set. Still — and this is important! — no reps were missed by going to failure.

Be conservative about your poundage increases. If you're patient, periodization will take you a long, long way—probably further than you ever dreamed possible. *Photo by John Balik.*

The phase ended as planned, with a new personal record. Our lifter makes a note in this training diary to aim for 20 reps with 220 in the next endurance phase. It's a good idea to record your goal in this way while the feel of the weight is fresh in your mind. When this phase comes around again, more than two months later, you'll be glad you did.

One more thing: Don't be discouraged because there's only a 10-pound gain here. In the long run, it's better to be conservative about your increases. After all, a five percent increase on each phase, if you lift for any time at all, soon will have you lifting incredible poundages! With periodization, patience will take you a long, long way... probably further than you ever dreamed possible.

THE STRENGTH AND ENDURANCE PHASE

Week Five
 Monday — Heavy (100%)
  Squats: 135 x 8 (warm-up)
        175 x 6 (warm-up)
        205 x 12 (work set)

We'll assume that our lifter's best Squat poundage at this lower number of reps — 12 — is 235. A person's maximum poundages as the reps decrease don't necessarily fall into a neat geometric progression. That is to say, some people are at their best lifting a heavy weight for a few repetitions, and others excel in the high repetition ranges. In other words, some people who can Squat 200 for 20 reps (like our imaginary lifter before the endurance phase just completed) will be capable of 12 repetitions with 235 pounds. Others, with the same 20-rep max, will be able to do more than 235 pounds or less. It's partly a matter of genetics and partly the number of reps you're used to doing. You'll probably be strongest in the repetition range you have practiced the most. The results of training are specific to the part of the muscle being stressed. Of course, that's why it's necessary to stress all components — with high, medium and low reps.

112

If you don't already know your strength in various repetition ranges, you'll have to find out by experimenting. After you go through the training phases once or twice, you'll basically know your capabilities. In the case of this lifter, I've assumed a 15-20 percent increase in his maximum for 12 reps versus 20. There's nothing magical about that percentage, but it's probably in the ballpark for the average person.

If you're surprised that I'm starting this phase with less than the poundage used at the end of the endurance phase, let me explain that it's important to start each phase with a weight you can handle fairly comfortably. After all, our lifter really put out at the end of the last phase, and his mind and body need a break. Starting with a moderate poundage allows you to experience a good momentum and strength buildup as the phase proceeds. Just as importantly, it also puts you on the track to exceed your previous 12-rep best. That's your goal, to lift a little more at the end of the phase than you've ever done before. Remember, the purpose of training in cycles is to *keep you progressing*.

Remember, too, that you do the exercise in a different fashion during this phase. In the endurance phase, you do slow, continuous reps without a pause; you want to build up lactic acid and stress the mitochondrial component of the muscles. Here you want to place greater stress on the contractile fibers, the myofibrils. So you perform the exercise a little faster, and you pause between reps to prevent lactic acid buildup.

However, you still maintain control of the weight at all times. As I've said before, you should never jerk or throw the weight. That takes the stress off the muscle and defeats your purpose. It's important to make the muscle contract all the way through the movement. Here the idea is to lift a little faster than in the endurance phase, but not so fast that you can't feel the muscle contract through the entire range of motion.

Also, it's important that you maintain proper body position at all times, so the stress stays focused on the body part being worked. This is especially true in the case of the Squat. When squatting, keep your torso upright and don't allow your back to round. Squat down slowly, under control, until your thighs are a

This is proper Squat position. Note in particular how straight I hold my back. Don't allow your back to round and never go down fast and bounce out of the bottom position. If you have a tendency to lean forward and bend your back, place a one inch (or less) piece of wood under your heels for balance. *Photo by Guy Appelman.*

little below parallel, and then come up strongly. Never go down fast and bounce out of the bottom position; that's inviting injury to your lower back and knees, and takes the stress off the thighs.

Again, in all phases and on all exercises, it's important that you maintain your body position and control the weight throughout the range of motion, both lifting and lowering.*

Now let's go on to the second Squat session of the fifth week.

* Cheating, of course, does have a place in bodybuilding — see *Ripped 2*, p. 65. But not in the Squat or other exercises where it can lead to injury.

Thursday — Light (85%)
Squats: 135 x 8 (warm-up)
                175 x 12 (work set)

Note that we dropped a warm-up set here. I'll repeat what I said about warm-up in *Ripped 2*: "Warming up increases the elasticity of the tendons and ligaments and causes a rise in the temperature of the muscle cells. It's a safeguard against injury. A cold muscle simply isn't prepared to perform up to capacity. A warm-up is important, but it shouldn't tire you out. Warm up, but don't overdo it. Save your energy for the sets that count, the heavy sets." In short, on this light day, a second warm-up set would serve no useful purpose. When you've been training for a while, you'll have a feel for how much warm-up is necessary. You won't need a calculator or stop watch. Your body will tell you what's right.

Week Six
Monday — Heavy (100%)
Squats: 135 x 8 (warm-up)
                185 x 6 (warm-up)
                220 x 12 (work set)

After taking a breather during week five, we start increasing the weight here, but not too fast. The work sets are a little harder; there's still plenty of room for progess, however.

Thursday — Light (85%)
Squats: 135 x 8 (warm-up)
                175 x 6 (warm-up)
                190 x 12 (work set)

Week Seven
Monday — Heavy (100%)
Squats: 135 x 8 (warm-up)
                185 x 6 (warm-up)
                205 x 4 (warm-up)
                235 x 12 (work set)

There's an extra warm-up set here, because the work set is

heavier. Our lifter equals his previous max. It went well and, as planned, a new record is in the cards for next week.

    Thursday — Light (85%)
        Squats: 135 x 8 (warm-up)
                        185 x 6 (warm-up)
                        200 x 12 (work set)

Week Eight
    Monday — Heavy (100%)
        Squats: 135 x 8 (warm-up)
                        185 x 6 (warm-up)
                        205 x 4 (warm-up)
                        225 x 3 (warm-up)
                        245 x 14 (work set) — personal record!

    Another PR, and two extra reps to boot. Great job! Our lifter ends the phase on a high note. Again, he was careful not to miss a rep by going to failure. In the next strength and endurance phase, 12 reps with 255 or 260 will be a cinch. Success, combined with patience, breeds success.

    Thursday — Light (85%)
        Squats: 135 x 8 (warm-up)
                        190 x 6 (warm-up)
                        210 x 12 (work set)

THE STRENGTH PHASE

Week Nine
    Monday — Heavy (100%)
        Squats: 135 x 8 (warm-up)
                        185 x 6 (warm-up)
                        215 x 4 (warm-up)
                        235 x 8 (work set)

    Our lifter's best (thus far) for eight reps in the Squat is 255. We decide to make eight reps at 265 pounds our end-of-cycle target,

116

which is realistic in view of the increases made during the first two phases. Again, we start out easy, taking a breather after the record-setting previous week, pacing our lifter for another PR in the 12th week.

As in the second phase, the lifter pauses between reps. But in this phase he thinks about exploding up with the weight on each rep. The weight is heavy enough, however, that it won't actually come up very fast. Think speed, but always *controlled* speed. As before, maintain your body position, and never jerk or throw the weight.

The reason for the emphasis on speed in this phase is to stimulate the central nervous system. You're training your brain to recruit the maximum possible number of contractile fibers, especially the fast-twitch variety, which increase in size most readily. (When the fast-twitch fibers contract, the slow-twitch fibers contract as well; see *The Lean Advantage*, p. 149.)

Remember what I said in *Ripped 2*: "Muscle fibers that aren't used remain small and weak; they fail to develop.... On the other hand, muscle fibers that are stimulated strongly hypertrophy; they grow bigger and stronger." Moreover, as I pointed out earlier, Dr. Mike Stone says that muscular endurance largely depends on the maximum strength level of the muscles being used. Strengthening additional fibers in this phase provides the base needed to lift more in the next endurance phase. With each trip through the whole cycle, you grow bigger and stronger.

Thursday — Light (85%)
Squats: 135 x 8 (warm-up)
             175 x 6 (warm-up)
             200 x 8 (work set)

Week 10
Monday — Heavy (100%)
Squats: 135 x 8 (warm-up)
             185 x 6 (warm-up)
             205 x 4 (warm-up)
             225 x 3 (warm-up)
             245 x 8 (work set)

Thursday — Light (85%)
Squats: 135 x 8 (warm-up)
               185 x 6 (warm-up)
               210 x 8 (work set)

Week 11

Monday — Heavy (100%)
Squats: 135 x 8 (warm-up)
               185 x 6 (warm-up)
               215 x 4 (warm-up)
               235 x 3 (warm-up)
               255 x 8 (work set)

The lifter equals his previous best (eight reps with 255 pounds) during this third week of the phase, and he's confident a new eight-rep PR will be established the next week.

Thursday — Light (85%)
Squats: 135 x 8 (warm-up)
               185 x 6 (warm-up)
               215 x 8 (work set)

Week 12

Monday — Heavy (100%)
Squats: 135 x 8 (warm-up)
               185 x 6 (warm-up)
               225 x 4 (warm-up)
               245 x 3 (warm-up)
               265 x 10 (work set) — personal best.

A perfect ending. When the next strength phase comes around, our lifter looks good for 275 or 280. But now it's time for a light day, and then a couple of easy weeks.

Thursday — Light (85%)
Squats: 135 x 8 (warm-up)
               185 x 6 (warm-up)
               205 x 4 (warm-up)
               225 x 8 (work set)

The active rest phase is very important to the strength and muscle-building process. Go to the beach or do something else you enjoy. *Photo by Bill Reynolds.*

THE RECOVERY PERIOD

This is the time for what Dr. Stone calls "active rest." Listen to what he says: "If an athlete simply moves right into hard training after peaking or after a season playing some sport, progress will be diminished. Complete rest, while sometimes necessary, also does not seem to produce as good a result as active rest. Active rest refers to participating in some other sport or occasionally your own at very low volumes and intensities."

So take it easy, but do something. I usually walk a lot and play around with some different exercises, using very light weights. After a week or two, you'll be rarin' to get back into the gym.

THE ROUTINES: A QUICK LOOK

To give you a quick overview of the routines to come, I've set them out below in chart form. As you can see, there are four routines: 1) Three-Day, Whole-Body; 2) Four-Day, Push-Pull Split; 3) Three-Way Plus One Split; and 4) All-Component, Peaking Routine.

The most readily apparent difference is that there are more sets per body part in each succeeding routine. But as you will soon learn, there are other distinctions as well. The routines run the gamut from the simple to the complex.

Whatever your level of experience in bodybuilding, you're urged to read everything we have said about these routines. That's because the explanation of each routine includes concepts that have application beyond the particular routine itself. You'll discover that there's much more here than the usual beginner-intermediate-advanced sequence of workouts.

It's true that the routines become more advanced the further you go; nevertheless, there's something of value in each routine for almost everyone. For example, there are times when even the most advanced bodybuilder can benefit from the first routine; and, of course, the beginner, if he or she continues to train, will eventually want to try the peaking routine. Personally, I use them all from time to time. Because, as I've already said, the key to success in bodybuilding training is variety.

120

WORK SETS PER BODY PART IN EACH ROUTINE

BODY PARTS	Three-Day, Whole-Body		Four-Day, Push-Pull Split	Three-Way Plus One Split		All-Component, Peaking	
	A	B		A	B	A	B
Frontal Thighs	1	2	4	5	3	7	3
Lower Back	1	2	2	1	0	1	0
Leg Biceps	0	2	2	3	1	3	1
Calf	2	2	4	6	3	6	3
Upper Back	2	2	4	6	4	8	4
Chest	2	2	4	6	4	8	4
Shoulders	2	2	4	6	4	8	4
Triceps	2	2	4	5	4	6	4
Biceps	2	2	4	4	3	6	3
Upper Abdominals	2	0	2	3	2	4	2
Lower Abdominals	0	2	2	3	2	4	2
Sides	1	0	2	3	2	4	2

Now let's examine each routine and see what it has to offer.

THREE-DAY, WHOLE-BODY ROUTINE

Don't take this routine lightly. It's a no-frills, simple routine, but it's by no means a cakewalk. It should not be attempted until you've spent at least a month or more on a beginner's routine (like the one in *Ripped 2*), conditioning your body to the stress of weight training. What's more, even if you've been training for years, you can still benefit from this routine. After more than 30 years of training, I still go on a routine like this occasionally.

As a matter of fact, in 1983 I experienced some of my best-ever results on a routine very similar to this. The reason, I think, was rest. A major plus of a routine like this is the rest it provides. As you may remember, in *Ripped 2* I've got a section titled "Rest Is Important." This routine certainly gives you a lot of rest. And for beginner and expert alike, rest — at times — can make the difference between success and failure.

As the name implies, this routine calls for three workouts a week, and you train the whole body each session. It's the kind of routine most people follow when they begin weight training. This, however, is a periodization routine, and that sets it apart from the usual beginner's program.

Like most three-day routines, this program is made up primarily of compound exercises, i.e., exercises which work several muscle groups simultaneously. Jan and Terry Todd call them the "multiple-muscle exercises." The best examples are the Squat and Deadlift. The first two exercises in the routine, they involve the hips, lower back and thighs, plus many other stabilizing and balancing muscles. Because they stress so many muscles (in fact, the biggest and strongest muscles in the body), these two exercises promote overall muscle growth and development. For that reason, they're probably the most productive exercises you can do. The drawback is that, when done properly, they're brutally hard.

To a lesser degree, the Bent-Over Row, Lat Pulldown, Bench Press, Dip, Press Behind Neck and Dumbbell Press — the other compound exercises included — have a similar overall muscular effect. Each exercise works a number of important but smaller muscles. When you train the whole body in one session, there's no room for anything but the best and most productive exercises — in other words, the com-

After more than 30 years of training, I still get good results from a three-day, whole-body routine like the one included here. *Photo by Guy Appelman.*

This is the correct starting position for the Deadlift. Note that I hold my back straight, just like I did on the squat. Pull with the legs and keep your back straight as you come erect with the weight. *Photo by Mike Neveux.*

pound or multiple-muscle exercises which make up practically the whole of this routine. You'll see that they're also the bedrock of the other routines in this book.

This routine includes only one exercise per body part, and only one or two work sets per exercise. That's because we're working the whole body in one session, and there isn't time and energy for more exercises and sets. This also means you have only one or two opportunities to stimulate each body part; therefore, it's essential that you concentrate and do your best on every set. Actually, that's the way you should approach every weight workout. Merely going through the motions rarely, if ever, produces much in the way of results.

The workouts in this routine take approximately an hour to complete. That's about the ideal length for a training session. If you go much over an hour, you'll probably lose your training drive. Why do that? You can get a lot done in an hour if you're industrious in the gym.

However, there's no need to hurry. As I said earlier, rest long enough to prepare for the next set, but don't allow yourself to cool off or lose training momentum. If you want something to go by, rest periods generally should run from three to four minutes after a heavy set of Squats or Deadlifts, and they may be as short as a minute or less after Curls.

You'll notice this routine consists of two workouts, A and B. Workout A is done twice a week, once heavy and once light. Workout A is the main routine; it's the one in which you'll be seeking to increase your personal best in the fourth week of each phase. Workout B is performed only once, with medium intensity; it provides variety.

Like all periodization programs, this routine features the hard-day/easy-day approach. As stated earlier, research has shown that it's best not to go heavy on a given exercise more than once a week. But it's also important to do each exercise a second time each week with less than maximum intensity. In line with that concept, workout A is performed on Day One and again on Day Five, using 100 percent in the first session and dropping back to 80 percent in the second. Workout B, the secondary routine, is done on Day Three only, with 90 percent intensity. Under this system, a different poundage or exercise is used each training day. That makes the training more interesting.

The B workout is important even though it's never done with maximum intensity. As I said earlier, because of time and energy limitations, a whole-body routine must be kept short and simple. This means you can't train the muscles from as many angles as you would like. The second routine makes up for this somewhat by stressing the body in ways that wouldn't be feasible if you did the same routine all three training days. Increase the poundages on the B workout in conjunction with the main workout, taking care to keep the intensity moderately hard through each phase.

You should, of course, decrease the reps and alter the exercise performance mode from phase to phase as previously described. So there will be no confusion, let me repeat the periodization sequence I recommend for bodybuilders: weeks one through four, do sets of 15 to 25 slow, continuous reps; in weeks four to eight, do 10 to 15 moderate-speed reps, pausing after each rep; and in the final four weeks, nine through 12, do six to 10 fast but controlled reps, pausing after each rep once again. Take a one- or two-week break after that, and then start the whole cycle over again, this time with slightly heavier weights than you used initially.

As we demonstrated earlier, using the Squat as an example, your goal is to end each phase by being able to handle a little more weight than you could at the end of the previous phase. Therefore, you should start each phase with poundages that will allow you to gradually increase each week and end up with a new personal best for that number of reps in the fourth week. I suggest that you begin each phase with about 15 percent less than your target weight, then increase about five percent each week. In other words, start with 85 percent of the top weight you plan to do in each exercise during that phase, go to 90 percent in the second week, 95 percent in the third and 100 percent in the last week. I usually plan to equal my previous record in the third week and establish a new PR in the last week.

In the two split routines coming up, you will be following the same approach (planning the same increases, going through the same rep and exercise style sequence, etc.). As will be explained later, the approach in the all-component peaking routine is slightly different.

Here's the full Three-Day, Whole-Body routine:

126

DAY ONE:

WORKOUT A — HEAVY (100%)

Brief General Warm-Up: Arm Curl and Extension, Shoulder
Shrug, Arm Swing (forward and backward), Knee Lift, Toe Touch
and Free Squat

Squat:	warm-up and one work set
Deadlift:	warm-up and one work set
Standing Calf Raise:	warm-up and two work sets
Bent-Over Barbell Row:	warm-up and two work sets
Bench Press:	warm-up and two work sets
Press Behind Neck:	warm-up and two work sets
Lying Triceps Extension:	warm-up and two work sets

This is the starting position for the Bent-Over Barbell Row. Note that my knees are bent. Hold this position and pull the bar up to your upper abdominal region, right below the rib cage. Make your upper back muscles, your lats, do the work, not your arms or lower back.

Here's the correct finishing position. The Bent-Over Row, like the Squat and Deadlift, is an example of the growth-promoting, multiple-muscle exercises that make up practically the whole of this routine. *Photos by Guy Appelman.*

127

Barbell Curl:	warm-up and two work sets
Bent-Knee Sit-Up:	warm-up and two work sets
(Hold dumbbell on chest, if necessary, for added resistance.)	
Dumbbell Side Bend:	warm-up and one work set
Brief General Cool-Down:	Same as the general warm-up

DAY TWO:

REST DAY

DAY THREE:

WORKOUT B — MEDIUM HEAVY (90%)

Brief General Warm-Up:	Same as Day One
Back Hyperext. (see photo):	warm-up and two work sets
Leg Extension:	warm-up and two work sets
Leg Curl:	warm-up and two work sets
Seated Calf Raise:	warm-up and two work sets
Lat Pull-Down (front):	warm-up and two work sets
Parallel Bar Dip:	warm-up and two work sets
Seated Dumbbell Press:	warm-up and two work sets
Triceps Cable Pushdown:	warm-up and two work sets
Seated Dumbbell Curl:	warm-up and two work sets
Hip Curl (see photo):	warm-up and two work sets
(Use ankle weights, if necessary, for added resistance.)	
Brief General Cool-Down:	Same as the general warm-up

DAY FOUR:

REST DAY

DAY FIVE:

WORKOUT A — LIGHT (80%)
(Same as Day One, but with 80% intensity.)

128

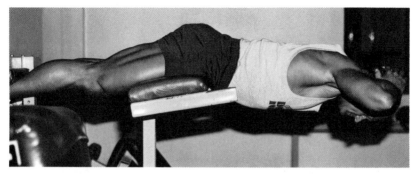

This is the finishing postion on the Back Hyperextension. This exercise works the lower back without compressing the spine. It's an example of the movements in Workout B which stress the body from different angles than Workout A. *Photo by Guy Appelman.*

Here's the finish position on the Hip Curl. Do this exercise correctly, and you'll really feel the action in your lower abdominal muscles. Start with your hips almost touching the incline board, and keeping the tension on your lower abs, curl your hips up toward your rib cage. If you feel the tension go off the lower abs, you have either lowered or raised your hips too much. Lower the angle of the board to reduce the resistance and add ankle weights to make it harder. *Photo by Mike Neveux.*

129

DAY SIX:

REST DAY

DAY SEVEN:

REST DAY

NOTE: It's beyond the scope of this book to explain how to perform basic exercises. If you need help in this area I recommend two books: *Keys to the Inner Universe* by Bill Pearl and *Secrets of Advanced Bodybuilders* by Health For Life. Pearl's book has the most complete list of exercises ever assembled. Each exercise is clearly explained with drawings and text. The second book, *Secrets,* has fewer exercises, but explains them in greater detail, providing valuable performance tips you won't find anywhere else. Both books are available from Ripped Enterprises.

FOUR-DAY, PUSH-PULL SPLIT

In this routine, the body is divided into pushing and pulling muscles, which allows time and energy to train each body part more completely. As you probably know, that's the purpose of a split routine; it permits you to concentrate more on each body part, do more sets or train each muscle group from more angles.

Here the pushing muscles — thighs, calves, chest, shoulders and triceps — are trained one day and the pulling muscles — lower back, leg biceps, upper back, biceps and abs — the next day. To complete the four-day training cycle, the pushing and pulling muscles are trained a second time each week, again on separate days, but with less intensity.

To spread the effort evenly over the course of the week and allow more complete recovery, the heavy sessions are scheduled on Day One and Day Five, with the lighter sessions in between on the second and fourth days of the training week. In other words, a

130

hard-day/easy-day sequence is maintained throughout the week.

You'll notice that in this and the other routines, I have numbered the training days rather than using days of the week. This allows you to fit the training sequence into your own schedule. In other words, Day One can fall on Monday or Friday or any other day (it's up to you). I usually schedule heavy sessions on days of the week when I typically have the most time to train.

I prefer the push-pull split over the more common upper- and lower-body split, because it spreads the effort more evenly between the two training days. A disadvantage of the upper- and lower-body split is that the legs and lower back, which take a tremendous amount of energy to train, are worked together. On a push-pull split, however, these two large body parts are trained on separate days, which makes for a more even division of labor.

An advantage common to both split routines is that muscles related to each other, i.e., muscles that work together, are trained on the same day. This allows half of the muscle groups to rest while the other half are being exercised. In the upper/lower body split, the upper body is allowed to recuperate on the days when the lower body is trained, and vice versa. In the push-pull split, the pulling muscles rest while the pushing muscles are trained, and the other way around. For example, the chest, shoulders and triceps work together, so they're trained together. By the same token, the lats and biceps work as a unit and they're trained together as well.

Admittedly, with the push-pull split, there is some overlap when Squats are done on the push day and Deadlifts on the pull day. The thighs, hips and lower back muscles are involved in both exercises and, therefore, are stressed on both days of this split. Nevertheless, I've found that it's better to do these two major exercises on separate days, rather than doing them together as part of a lower-body day. There are two very practical reasons for this: energy and enthusiasm. When Squats and Deadlifts are done together, there's not much energy left over for other exercises. Plus, it's much easier, mentally, to face these two tough exercises when they're done in separate sessions. Split them up and you'll be more enthusiastic and put more intensity into each one. Also, the rest of the particular workout will go better as well.

131

The purpose of a split routine is to allow you to concentrate more on each body part. *Photo by John Balik.*

As I said earlier, Deadlifts, when done properly, are brutally hard. Wrist straps make them a little easier by securing the grip. After all, the Deadlift is a back and leg exercise, not a forearm exercise. I recommend straps in any exercise where hand strength tends to fail, making the exercise less effective.

You can see that my straps get plenty of use. You can buy straps ready-made or, like me, you can have them custom-made at a canvas and upholstering shop. Mine were made with seat belt material. *Photos by Guy Appelman.*

Doing Squats and Deadlifts on separate days, as recommended here, is contrary to the basically sound philosophy of pairing body parts that function together, but it works nevertheless. Power-lifters almost always do the Squat and Deadlift on different days; it works for them. Try it; it'll work for you, too.

One more thing: I like anchoring training sessions to either the Squat or the Deadlift. As pointed out earlier, these two exercises stimulate the whole body to grow; they're probably the most effective exercises, from a whole-body standpoint, that you can do. I believe both halves of the push-pull split are more productive when they include one of these growth-stimulating exercises.

As might be expected, this four-day split routine has roughly twice as many work sets for each body part as the previous routine. The whole-body routine had only one exercise per body part in each session. Here, to work the muscles from more than one angle, two or more exercises are included for most body parts.

Still, in keeping with my overall emphasis on variety, only one or two work sets are indicated for each exercise. I believe this yields the best results. Doing only a few sets of each exercise allows you to focus your concentration and do a better job. By contrast, when you perform many sets of an exercise, quality and intensity almost always suffer. Consciously or unconsciously, you hold back in the early sets, and then you're too tired to do the final sets with maximum intensity. Most people, I believe, do best when they focus their efforts on one or two sets of each exercise.

For much the same reason, I don't like doing an exercise a second time with the same weight and reps. I prefer to change the weight or reps on each set. For example, during the high-rep endurance phase, I frequently do the first set with a weight that allows 15 reps, and then decrease the weight so I can do 20 reps on the second work set. This makes training more interesting and productive. I suggest that you follow the same pattern. However, be sure to stay within the repetition range called for in that training phase.

To illustrate further, during the strength-endurance phase, I usually do 10 reps on the first set and 12-15 reps on the second set with a lighter weight. Six reps on the first set and 8-10 reps on the second set works well during the strength phase. Of course, I

134

always warm up before doing the first, and heaviest, set.

The heaviest set is done first for a reason. If you do the high-rep set first, lactic acid buildup (or the pump) may prevent the contractile fibers from working maximally on the next set. So I suggest that you do the set that produces the most pump last.

An important reminder before we look at the routine itself: Be sure to back off to 85 percent on Day Two and Day Four. This allows better recovery; you'll gain faster this way than if you try to go heavy each workout. You'll also enjoy your training more.

DAY ONE

PUSHING MUSCLES — HEAVY (100%)

Brief General Warm-Up:	Same as before
Squat:	warm-up and two work sets
Leg Extension:	warm-up and two work sets
Standing Calf Raise:	warm-up and two work sets
Seated Calf Raise:	warm-up and two work sets
Bench Press:	warm-up and two work sets
Incline Dumbbell Press:	warm-up and one work set
Crossover Pulley Fly:	warm-up and one work set
Press Behind Neck:	warm-up and two work sets
Dumbbell Lateral Raise:	warm-up and two work sets
Triceps Cable Pushdown:	warm-up and two work sets
Dumbbell Behind-Neck Triceps Extension:	warm-up and two work sets
Brief General Cool-Down:	Same as general warm-up

DAY TWO

PULLING MUSCLES — LIGHT (85%)

Brief General Warm-Up:	Same as before
Deadlift:	warm-up and two work sets
Leg Curl:	warm-up and two work sets

Lat Pulldown (Front):	warm-up and two work sets
Bent-Over Barbell Row:	warm-up and two work sets
Barbell Curl:	warm-up and two work sets
Preacher-Bench	
Barbell Curl:	warm-up and two work sets
Bent-Knee Sit-Up:	warm-up and two work sets
Hip Curl:	warm-up and two work sets
Dumbbell Side Bends:	warm-up and two work sets
Brief General Cool-Down:	Same as general warm-up

DAY THREE

REST DAY

DAY FOUR

PUSHING MUSCLES — SAME AS DAY ONE, BUT LIGHT
(85%)

DAY FIVE

PULLING MUSCLES — SAME AS DAY TWO, BUT HEAVY
(100%)

DAY SIX

REST DAY

DAY SEVEN

REST DAY

The Standing Barbell Curl is probably the single best exercise for the biceps. It's included in all the routines. I'm using a cambered bar or E-Z Curl Bar here because it's easier on the elbows.

This routine adds the Preacher Bench Curl, shown here, which provides more resistance than the regular Barbell Curl at the beginning of the exercise. Working each body part from a variety of angles gives you more complete development. It's also more fun than doing the same exercise all the time. Don't expect to change the basic shape of your muscles, however. For example, if nature gave you short biceps, Preacher Curls won't give you long biceps like Larry Scott. *Photos by Guy Appelman.*

The Bench Press is the basic exercise for the chest. This routine adds the Incline Dumbbell Press, shown here, to place extra stress on the upper chest muscles.

The Crossover Pulley Fly, shown here, is added to stress the lower chest muscles. *Photos by Guy Appelman.*

Incline Presses can also be done with a barbell and at different angles of incline. I like to keep the bench pretty far down, about 45°. If the angle is too steep, you work the deltoids more than the chest. *Photo by Wayne Gallasch.*

138

THREE-WAY SPLIT PLUS ONE

This is my favorite routine; it's the one I use most often. Among the advantages of the three-way split, of course, is that it allows time for more work on each body part. There's roughly 50 percent more work sets and exercises here than in the last routine. At least that's the case for most body parts.

The only exceptions are the arms, lower back and frontal thighs. Fewer direct sets have been added for these body parts. The triceps and biceps are small, uncomplicated muscles which receive extra work when the chest and upper back are trained; thus, it isn't necessary to increase the direct sets for them by 50 percent.

There's a similar reason for limiting the additional exercises for the lower back and quads. In this routine we get double duty out of the Squat and Deadlift. Although it's primarily a lower back exercise, the Deadlift affects the thighs strongly. And the Squat, primarily a thigh exercise, also affects the lower back. So, if we count Squats among the exercises for the lower back, there are, in effect, 50 percent more sets for that body part. Likewise, if you count Deadlifts as a thigh exercise, this routine, in fact, has 50 percent more sets for the quads.

This works out well because it's tough to face a lot of work sets in these two brutally hard exercises. After you try it, I think you'll agree that two hard sets of Squats and one on the Deadlift, plus a hard set of Leg Presses and two more on the Leg Extension, is more than enough stimulation for the lower back and quads. After all, working out is supposed to be fun, not something you dread.

Another advantage of this particular three-way split is that the leg day falls between the upper back/chest day and the shoulder/ arm day. This allows an extra day for the upper body to recover. That's important because many splits train upper body parts on consecutive days, which causes excessive fatigue in the shoulders and arms. The deltoids, biceps and triceps get a double dose of work; they're worked once directly, and then again, indirectly, as helping muscles (synergists) when the upper back and chest are trained. I used to wonder why my deltoids were tired all the time. I figured it out when the fatigue disappeared after I switched to this split.

The Three-Way Plus One is my favorite split. It gives each body part plenty of work, but still keeps workouts short enough that intensity can be maintained. *Photo by John Balik.*

Day Six, when the whole body is trained at 85% intensity, is a crucial part of this routine. Research has shown that best progress is made when an exercise is performed hard once and again easy each week. *Photo by Bill Reynolds.*

A unique feature of this routine is that the entire body is trained on Day Six! That's done to accommodate the hard-day/easy-day training principle. As I've already said several times, research shows you make the best progress when you do an exercise hard and then easy each week. My own experience confirms this. There is a problem, however, fitting both the three-way split and the heavy-day, light-day approach into a seven-day week. Most of us prefer to have our given workouts fall on the same day each week, rather than on different days. The latter, of course, would be the case if the three-day training sequence was repeated after a rest day. I decided to try solving this problem by training the whole body light on a single day, which would allow me to fit the whole program into a seven-day pattern. Happily, I found that this works fine.

My worry, of course, was that doing *all* the exercises from a three-way split on a single day would be too much — even at 85 percent intensity. Well, it's not. A few adjustments were required, however.

First, I did only one set of each exercise. Next, I dropped the Deadlift from the whole-body program on Day Six, because experience — mine and that of others — proves that it takes a week of complete rest to recover from a heavy Deadlift session. I also scheduled Leg Curls and Leg Extensions first in the routine to reduce the warm-up sets required on the Squat. When the quadriceps and leg biceps are warmed up beforehand, only one warm-up set is necessary on Squats. Of course, the fact that you're training at only 85 percent intensity also reduces the need for warm-up sets.

Indeed, except for the Squat, I found that warm-up sets aren't necessary on this light day. You may have different warm-up requirements, however. So experiment to determine your individual warm-up needs. It's better to be safe than sorry. By all means, when in doubt, do a warm-up set or two.

Most people, I think, will feel fine doing the 85 percent sets all in one session. You'll probably find that you can complete this light workout in about 75 minutes. What's more, you'll enjoy it. With 85 percent poundages, you can concentrate on getting a full stretch and contraction on every rep. It's a great feeling!

Here's the complete routine:

DAY ONE

UPPER BACK, CHEST AND UPPER ABS — HEAVY (100%)

Brief General Warm-Up:	Same as before
Narrow-Grip Lat Pulldown:	warm-up and two work sets
Bent-Over, Two-Arm	
Dumbbell Row:	warm-up and two work sets
Behind-Neck Lat	
Pulldown:	warm-up and one work set
Seated Long Cable Row:	warm-up and one work set
Bench Press:	warm-up and two work sets
Incline Dumbbell Press:	warm-up and two work sets
Parallel Bar Dip:	warm-up and one work set
Crossover Pulley Fly:	warm-up and one work set
Bent-Knee Sit-Up:	warm-up and two work sets
Kneeling Ab Cable	
Pulldown (see photo page 162):	warm-up and one work set
Brief General Cool-Down:	Same as general warm-up

DAY TWO

THIGHS, LOWER BACK, CALVES AND OBLIQUES — HEAVY (100%)

Brief General Warm-Up:	Same as before
Squat:	warm-up and two work sets
Deadlift:	warm-up and one work set
Leg Press:	warm-up and one work set
Leg Extension:	warm-up and two work sets
Leg Curl:	warm-up and three work sets
Standing Calf Raise:	warm-up and two work sets
Seated Calf Raise:	warm-up and two work sets
Calf Raise on Leg Press:	warm-up and two work sets
Dumbbell Side Bend:	warm-up and two work sets
Sit-Up to Side on Steep	warm-up and one work set
Incline (see photo):	(alternate side to side)
Brief General Cool-Down:	Same as general warm-up

DAY THREE

SHOULDERS, TRICEPS, BICEPS AND LOWER ABS — HEAVY (100%)

Brief General Warm-Up:	Same as before
2-Arm Dumbbell Upright Row:	warm-up and two work sets
Behind-Neck Press:	warm-up and two work sets
Dumbbell Side Lateral Raise:	warm-up and one work set
Seated Dumbbell Press:	warm-up and one work set
Narrow-Grip Bench Press:	warm-up and two work sets
Triceps Cable Pushdown:	warm-up and one work set
Dumbbell Behind-Neck Triceps Extension:	warm-up and one work set
Dumbbell Triceps Kickback:	warm-up and one work set
Barbell Curl:	warm-up and two work sets
Preacher-Bench Barbell Curl:	warm-up and one work set
Dumbbell Curl on Incline Bench:	warm-up and one work set
Hip Curl:	warm-up and two work sets
Hanging Leg Raise:	warm-up and one work set
Brief General Cool-Down:	Same as general warm-up

DAY FOUR

REST DAY

DAY FIVE

REST DAY

DAY SIX

WHOLE BODY — LIGHT (85%)

Brief General Warm-Up:	Same as before
Leg Curl:	one work set
Leg Extension:	one work set
Squat:	warm-up and one work set

144

Leg Press:	one work set
Standing Calf Raise:	one work set
Seated Calf Raise:	one work set
Calf Raise on Leg Press:	one work set
Narrow-Grip Lat Pulldown:	one work set
Bent-Over, Two-Arm Dumbbell Row:	one work set
Behind-Neck Lat Pulldown:	one work set
Seated Long Cable Row:	one work set
Bench Press:	one work set
Dumbbell Press on Incline Bench:	one work set
Parallel Bar Dip:	one work set
Crossover Pulley Fly:	one work set
Two-Arm Dumbbell Upright Row:	one work set
Behind-Neck Press:	one work set
Dumbbell Side Lateral Raise:	one work set
Seated Dumbbell Press:	one work set
Narrow-Grip Bench Press:	one work set
Triceps Cable Pushdown:	one work set
Dumbbell Behind-Neck Triceps Extension:	one work set
Dumbbell Triceps Kickback:	one work set
Barbell Curl:	one work set
Barbell Curl on Preacher Bench:	one work set
Dumbbell Curl in Incline Bench:	one work set
Hip Curl:	one work set
Hanging Leg Raise:	one work set
Bent-Knee Sit-Up:	one work set
Kneeling Ab Cable Pulldown:	one work set
Dumbbell Side Bend:	one work set
Sit-Up to Side on Steep Incline:	one work set (alternate side to side)
Brief General Cool-Down:	Same as general warm-up

SPECIAL NOTE: *If you need warm-up sets on any exercise, do them — whether or not they're indicated above.*

DAY SEVEN

REST DAY

Several new upper back exercises are included in this routine. The Narrow-Grip Lat Pulldown, shown here, is one. It's one of the best lat exercises because, done properly, it stresses the majority of the upper back muscles. Stretch your lats at the start like this.

Gradually lean back and pull down to the sternum as shown here. Pull with your back mucles, not your arms, and squeeze your shoulder blades together at the bottom.

As you can see in this photo, the rear deltoids are also affected strongly. That's true in most upper back exercises. In fact, if you focus on it, you'll notice that your rear deltoids are tired when you finish training your lats. That's why I don't include separate exercises for the rear deltoids in any of the routines.

Likewise, the front deltoids get plenty of work on chest exercises. So I don't include separate exercises for the front delts either. *Photos by Guy Appelman.*

146

In this routine dumbbells are substituted for the barbell on Bent-Over Rows. There are several variations of this exercise. Here I'm doing Dumbbell Rows leaning over the back of an incline bench. This cuts down on cheating and takes the stress off the lower back.

Usually, however, I do Dumbbell Rows without the bench. The position is the same as shown on page 127. I like Dumbbell Rows because you can stretch more at the start and pull the weight higher.

This is the finish. Remember to pull with your back muscles, not your arms. *Photos by Guy Appelman.*

147

Another variation is the One-Arm Dumbbell Row shown here. Support yourself with the free hand. Let the Dumbbell come down across your body, by your opposite foot, to stretch the lat fully at the start.

Seated Long Cable Rows are also included in this routine. Keep lower back involvement to a minimum. Stretch at the start and pull with your lats. *Photos by Guy Appelman.*

Three calf exercises are included on Day Two. The Standing Calf Raise, shown here, is probably the single best exercise for the calves. Come all the way up on your toes and contract your calves hard.

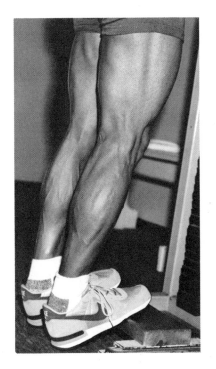

Stretch all the way down at the bottom like this. *Photos by Guy Appelman.*

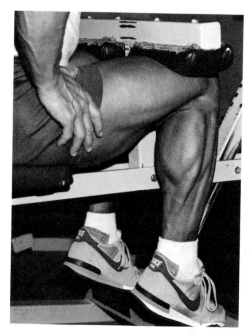

The Seated Calf Raise, shown here, works the underlying soleus muscle very effectively.

The Calf Raise on the Leg Press Machine shown here, is one of my favorites. There's no strain on the lower back and you can get a good stretch at the bottom and a great contraction at the top. *Photos by Guy Appelman.*

150

ALL-COMPONENT, PEAKING ROUTINE

This routine is tough! It's for use the last four weeks before a contest, or any other time you want to be at your absolute best. The reason it's called an "all-component" routine is because it places maximum stress on both the contractile and endurance components of the muscle cell. It forces the myofibrils and mitochondria to a peak of development simultaneously. In other words, it takes the features from all three phases of the Ripped Cycle System and puts them into one peaking phase.

The format here is the same as in the last routine. The difference is that each body part is trained with low, medium and high reps. All three exercise performance modes (fast, moderate and slow reps) are used to optimally stress all components of the muscle cell. The main exercise for each body part is done with sets of eight, 12 and 20 reps. The eight-rep set is the heaviest.

On this first set, do fast, controlled reps, pausing briefly between reps to avoid lactic acid buildup and place primary stress on the contractile fibers. On the second set, decrease the weight and do 12 repetitions. Perform them at moderate speed and, again, pause briefly between reps. On the final set, decrease the weight again and do 20 repetitions in slow, continuous-tension style. If necessary, it's okay to pause once or twice after you get to 10 reps. This final set, of course, is primarily for the mitochondria, the endurance component of the muscle cell. As you can see, doing three sets in this way will stress all components of the muscle cell.

The other exercises for each body part work the same muscles from different angles. You do 10 to 15 repetitions, using the same performance mode as in the strength and endurance phase, i.e., moderate speed with a pause between reps. Again, the idea is to stress both the strength and endurance components of the muscle cells, but without using all three repetition ranges and exercise performance modes. It's a compromise to keep the workout from getting entirely out of hand.

Day Six, the light day, is the same as in the last routine, except that you do 12 repetitions per set, again with 85 percent poundages. This is another compromise, because it wouldn't be practical to use low, medium and high reps, as well as three performance modes (fast, moderate, slow), on the light, whole-body day.

151

This routine, combined with proper diet (low sodium intake is very important), will bring your physique to a super peak. But I warn you, it's a killer. Be realistic in setting your poundage goals. Don't attempt to attain new highs here. If you can equal your best in all three rep ranges in the same workout, that's progress in anybody's book. Remember not to miss a single rep. Good luck! *Photo by Guy Appelman.*

That's it. Except for a warning: Don't follow this routine for more than four weeks. If you do, you'll become stale and over-trained. And one more thing: After four weeks on the routine, you'll need a week or two of active rest.

DAY ONE

UPPER BACK, CHEST AND UPPER ABS — HEAVY (100%)

Brief General Warm-Up:	Same as before
Narrow-Grip Lat Pulldown:	warm-up and three work sets/ 8, 12 and 20 reps
Bent-Over, 2-Arm Dumbbell Row:	warm-up and three work sets/ 8, 12 and 20 reps
Behind-Neck Lat Pulldown:	warm-up and one work set/ 12 reps
Seated Long Cable Row:	warm-up and one work set/ 12 reps
Bench Press:	warm-up and three work sets/ 8, 12 and 20 reps
Dumbbell Press on Incline Bench:	warm-up and three work sets/ 8, 12 and 20 reps
Parallel Bar Dip:	warm-up and one work set/ 12 reps
Crossover Pulley Fly:	warm-up and one work set/ 12 reps
Bent-Knee Sit-Up:	warm-up and two work sets/ 10 and 15 reps (hold weight on chest for added resistance, if necessary)
Kneeling Ab Cable Pulldown (see photo):	warm-up and two work sets/ 10 and 15 reps
Brief General Cool-Down:	Same as general warm-up

DAY TWO

THIGHS, LOWER BACK, CALVES AND OBLIQUES — HEAVY (100%)

Brief General Warm-Up:	Same as before
Squat:	warm-up and three work sets/ 8, 12 and 20 reps
Deadlift:	warm-up and one work set/ 10 reps
Leg Press:	warm-up and two work sets/ 10 and 15 reps
Leg Extension:	warm-up and two work sets/ 10 and 15 reps
Leg Curl:	warm-up and three work sets/ 8, 12 and 20 reps
Standing Calf Raise:	warm-up and three work sets/ 8, 12 and 20 reps
Seated Calf Raise:	warm-up and two work sets/ 10 and 15 reps
Calf Raise on Leg Press:	warm-up and one work set/ 12 reps
Dumbbell Side Bend:	warm-up and two work sets/ 10 and 15 reps
Sit-Ups to Side on Steep Incline (see photos):	warm-up and two work sets/ 12 and 16 reps (alternate side to side)
Brief General Cool-Down:	Same as warm-up

DAY THREE

SHOULDERS, TRICEPS, BICEPS AND LOWER ABS — HEAVY (100%)

Brief General Warm-Up:	Same as before
Two-Arm Dumbbell Upright Row:	warm-up and three work sets/ 8, 12 and 20 reps

Behind-Neck Press:	warm-up and three work sets/ 8, 12 and 20 reps
Dumbbell Side Lateral Raise:	warm-up and one work set/ 12 reps
Seated Dumbbell Press:	warm-up and one work set/ 12 reps
Narrow-Grip Bench Press:	warm-up and three work sets/ 8, 12 and 20 reps
Triceps Cable Pushdown:	warm-up and one work set/ 12 reps
Dumbbell Behind-Neck Triceps Extension:	warm-up and one work set/ 12 reps
Dumbbell Triceps Kickback:	warm-up and one work set/ 12 reps
Barbell Curl:	warm-up and three work sets/ 8, 12 and 20 reps
Barbell Curl on Preacher Bench:	warm-up and one work set/ 12 reps
Dumbbell Curl on Incline Bench:	warm-up and one work set/ 12 reps
Hip Curl:	warm-up and two work sets/ 10 and 15 reps
Hanging Leg Raise:	warm-up and two work sets/ 10 and 15 reps
Brief General Cool-Down:	Same as warm-up

DAY FOUR

REST DAY

DAY FIVE

REST DAY

DAY SIX

WHOLE BODY — LIGHT (85%)

Brief General Warm-Up:	Same as before
Leg Curl:	one work set/12 reps
Leg Extension:	one work set/12 reps
Squat:	warm-up and one work set/12 reps
Leg Press:	one work set/12 reps
Standing Calf Raise:	one work set/12 reps
Seated Calf Raise:	one work set/12 reps
Calf Raise on Leg Press:	one work set/12 reps
Narrow-Grip Lat Pulldown:	one work set/12 reps
Bent-Over, Two-Arm Dumbbell Row:	one work set/12 reps
Behind-Neck Lat Pulldown:	one work set/12 reps
Seated Long Cable Row:	one work set/12 reps
Bench Press:	one work set/12 reps
Dumbbell Press on Incline Bench:	one work set/12 reps
Parallel Bar Dip:	one work set/12 reps
Crossover Pulley Fly:	one work set/12 reps
Two-Arm Dumbbell Upright Row:	one work set/12 reps
Behind-Neck Press:	one work set/12 reps
Dumbbell Side Lateral Raise:	one work set/12 reps
Seated Dumbbell Press:	one work set/12 reps
Narrow-Grip Bench Press:	one work set/12 reps
Triceps Cable Pushdown:	one work set/12 reps
Dumbbell Behind-Neck Triceps Extension:	one work set/12 reps
Dumbbell Triceps Kickback:	one work set/12 reps
Barbell Curl:	one work set/12 reps
Barbell Curl on Preacher Bench:	one work set/12 reps
Dumbbell Curl in Incline Bench:	one work set/12 reps
Hip Curl:	one work set/12 reps
Hanging Leg Raise:	one work set/12 reps
Bent-Knee Sit-Up:	one work set/12 reps

Kneeling Ab Cable Pulldown:	one work set/12 reps
Dumbbell Side Bend:	one work set/12 reps
Sit-Up to Side on Steep Incline:	one work set/12 reps
	(alternate side to side)
Brief General Cool-Down:	Same as general warm-up

SPECIAL NOTE: *If you need warm-up sets on any exercise, do them — whether or not they're indicated above.*

DAY SEVEN

REST DAY

Here, as in the last routine, the main triceps exercise is the Narrow-Grip Bench Press. It hits the triceps squarely with some help from the chest and shoulders. The other triceps exercises are isolation movements which place the primary stress at different points in the range of motion. The first is the Triceps Cable Pushdown, shown here. The main stress on this exercise is in the middle of the range of motion, about half way down. It's easier at the start and finish. *Photo by Bill Reynolds.*

Dumbell Behind-Neck Triceps Extension is next. It places primary stress at the start of the motion. It can also be done with a pulley, as shown here.

This is near the finish of the movement. Pulleys provide resistance over a wider range of movement than free weights. That's because the weight stack is always pulling straight up and down. *Photos by Bill Reynolds.*

The Triceps Pushup, shown here, can also be substituted for the Dumbbell Behind-Neck Triceps extension. Bill Pearl showed me this movement. It's a lot harder than it looks. You vary the resistance by changing the height of the bar and your foot position. *Photo by Guy Appelman.*

159

The last triceps exercise is the Dumbbell Kickback. This is the starting position.

Here's the finish. Obviously, this exercise puts the main stress at the end of the movement. Keep your elbows lined up with your torso. If you rotate the palms up (pronate) more than I am here, you'll get a better contraction of the triceps, especially the long, inner head. *Photos by Guy Appelman.*

In this and the previous routine, the Dumbbell Curl on Incline Bench, shown here, is added as a third biceps exercise. You'll remember that the Barbell Curl is the main biceps exercise. Preacher Bench Curls are included to work the first part of the curling motion. Incline Curls round out the picture. As this photo clearly shows, they put the stress at the end of the curl, the fully contracted position. *Photo by Mike Neveux.*

Two exercises each are included for the upper abs, the lower abs and the sides. The Bent-Knee Sit-Up, shown here, is the best exercise I know for the upper abs. It's included in all the routines. Hold a weight on your chest for added resistance, if necessary. Be sure to keep your knees bent and curl your body up like a ball. Focus on shortening and lengthening the distance between your rib cage and your hips. *Photo by Guy Appelman.*

Here and in the last routine, the second upper ab movement, is the Kneeling Ab Cable Pulldown. This is the starting position. Simply pull your elbows to the floor, curling up as you do so. Hold the contraction at the bottom for a second or two and then come back up slowly. Make your abs work all the way, down and up. *Photo by Bill Reynolds.*

The Dumbbell Side Bend is included in every routine. I think it's the best exercise for the obliques. Don't worry about overdeveloping your side muscles. That's very unlikely. "Love handles" are almost always caused by excess fat over the obliques, not overly large muscles. *Photo by Guy Appelman.*

163

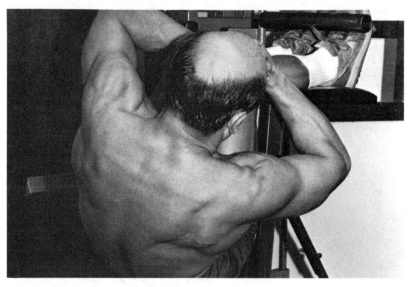

The Sit-Up to Side on Steep Incline is the second exercise for the sides. Here's how it's done: curl up on one side, lower on that side, and then repeat on the other side. Do this correctly and you'll really feel the action in your side muscles, as you raise and lower your body. Hold a dumbbell in your hands if you need more resistance. One more thing: be sure you use a stable, well-anchored decline bench. *Photos by Guy Appelman.*

The Hip Curl is included again. As you probably guessed, it's my favorite exercise for the lower abs. The finish position was shown earlier (Page 129). Here's the start. Note that my hips are almost, but not quite, touching the incline board. Keep tension on the lower abs throughout the movement. *Photo by Mike Neveux.*

The Hanging Leg Raise is the second lower ab exercise in this and the previous routine. As in the Hip Curl, curl your hips up, hold briefly in the position shown here, and then lower slowly. Try not to swing too much, because that takes the stress off the abs. After a while you may need ankle weights for added resistance. *Photo by Guy Appelman.*

165

THE AEROBICS PROBLEM/SOLUTION

Aerobics, for bodybuilders, presents a dilemma. Many bodybuilding oldtimers have long held the view that endurance training is bad for a bodybuilder. They say it destroys muscle tissue. But today's younger, scientifically-oriented iron pumpers, on the other hand, say that aerobic exercise is necessary to burn body fat and lower the fat setpoint.

It turns out there's truth in both views. The problem for bodybuilders is how to get the fat-burning benefits of aerobics without sacrificing hard-earned muscle tissue. Let's see if we can sort out this predicament and come up with some solutions.

I've already made the case for aerobics — at length in *Ripped 2* and *The Lean Advantage,* and briefly earlier in this book. So there's no point in repeating myself, except to say this: No doubt about it, bodybuilders need the aid of aerobic exercise to achieve maximum leanness. Here I'll focus on the drawbacks and how to avoid them.

Anyone can see that too much aerobic exercise can interfere with a bodybuilder's progress by creating so much fatigue that there's nothing left for weight workouts — I discussed that in *Ripped 2.* But it wasn't until I read the November 1983 issue of *The Physician and Sportsmedicine,* however, that I came upon the first, for me, scientific evidence that prolonged endurance exercise actually destroys muscle tissue. The details of that study are reported in *The Lean Advantage* (p. 118), but they're worth summarizing here since they heighten one's awareness of the aerobics problem for bodybuilders.

The study looked at 12 male runners during a 20-day road race. It showed that the increased mileage (double the regular training distance) that these individuals ran during that period produced thigh muscle atrophy. Significantly, they lost lean tissue, but not fat.

Still, it wasn't until later, when I read the book by Drs. Mike Stone and Harold O'Bryant referred to earlier, that I began to pay attention to the pitfalls of aerobic exercise in a major way. According to them, recent research suggests that aerobic exercise can cause a change in muscle fiber type! It seems that there exists a continuum of muscle fiber types ranging from the slowest to the fastest contracting, and that aerobic training can result in the formation of more slow-twitch fibers. Conversely, heavy weight training can bring about an increase in fast-twitch fibers.

Muscle fiber distribution is still thought to be governed largely by genetic factors, but there appears to be some fibers — fast-twitch glycolytic (FG) and fast-twitch oxidative glycolytic (FOG) fibers — that can take on fast-twitch or slow-twitch characteristics depending on the type of training they undergo. This is important to bodybuilders, because fast-twitch fibers increase in size (hypertrophy) much more than do slow-twitch fibers. (Both fiber types contain myofibrils and mitochondria.)

As a result of their training, endurance athletes appear to have a larger volume of slow-twitch fibers; sprinters, jumpers and weightlifters have a higher volume of fast-twitch fibers. The changes that take place in the muscles as a result of strength training appear to be considerably different than those resulting from aerobic exercise. As a matter of fact, Dr. Stone says (get this!) that the response to endurance and strength training are somewhat mutually exclusive, and that efforts to strive for excellence in both areas can be counterproductive.

In addition to changing fiber type from fast to slow, Dr. Stone says the research suggests that long-distance running and other prolonged endurance activities may affect various hormones in a manner which increases skeletal muscle catabolism (breakdown) resulting in a smaller muscle mass. It may also diminish muscle fiber recruitment and whole muscle contraction; of course, the extra activity of jogging, cycling, etc., may lead to overtraining.

In view of these negative effects of extended aerobic exercise, Stone and O'Bryant recommend that athletes interested in strength and muscle size use interval training. They say intervals will increase endurance without compromising muscle mass and power. As an example, they suggest that football players in summer training do sprints — 220s, 330s and 440s — with two- to four-minute rest intervals.

Bodybuilders, of course, are required to be leaner than football players. And since, of necessity, they'll be doing more aerobics, they need more specific guidance on incorporating aerobic exer-

Cory Everson, the odds-on favorite to win the Ms. Olympia title for a record third time in 1986, knows that too much aerobic exercise can run counter to muscle size. Even though she has a strong aerobic training background (she was a track and field champion while a student at the University of Wisconsin) she now does very little endurance training. When preparing to defend her title as the world's top female bodybuilder, she relies entirely on twice-a-day weight training to get ripped. Realize, however, that Cory is unusual. Her present muscle mass gives her a fast metabolism. Plus, her body fat is already quite low. At her stage of development, she may not need the proven fat-burning benefits of aerobic exercise. *Photo courtesy of Cory and Jeff Everson.*

cise into their training program.

Combining the research and recommendations of Stone and O'Bryant with common sense and my own experience, I've developed aerobic exercise guidelines for myself. I believe they'll help other bodybuilders as well. These guidelines are as follows:

1) Limit strenuous aerobic sessions to 30 minutes, excluding warm-up and cool-down, four times a week.

2) Practice different forms of aerobic exercise to distribute the stress to different parts of the body.

3) Include bursts of high-intensity muscular effort in every aerobic session.

What's the basic objective of these guidelines? Well, think back to the discussion earlier of the importance of exercise in getting ripped. What I said there, essentially, was that your body mirrors your lifestyle. If you train like a marathon runner, you'll probably end up looking like one — with small muscles suitable for running 26-plus miles. On the other hand, if you train like a weightlifter, you'll probably end up with big muscles suited for lifting heavy weights.

In these two extremes, the body receives a clear signal one way or the other: to adjust for endurance or for strength. The problem comes when the body gets competing, possibly mutually exclusive, messages; it doesn't know whether to adapt for endurance (slow-twitch fibers and small muscles) or strength (fast-twitch fibers and large muscles). So it does neither very well.

My guidelines are designed to allow enough aerobic exercise for fat-burning purposes without sending mixed messages to the muscles. Because the message you want to send to your body as a result of your training (both weights and aerobics) must be loud and clear: I'm a bodybuilder, not a marathoner; my lifestyle requires muscle — lean muscle.

For bodybuilders, therefore, I recommend a variety of relatively short and infrequent aerobic sessions interspersed with explosive muscular effort. Now let's examine these guidelines individually and see how each works in actual practice.

The first rule, of course, is designed to keep you from destroying muscle tissue like those 20-day road race participants. It's probably the most important guideline. It keeps you from overdosing on aerobics to the detriment of your bodybuilding progress.

I comply with the first rule — no more than four aerobic sessions a week — by scheduling aerobic sessions to coincide with weight sessions. I do aerobics and weights on the same day. I always lift first, however, because that's my primary activity. This works better than doing aerobics on the off days.

I realize that many people do weights and aerobics on alternate days, but that's a mistake. It doesn't allow time for complete recuperation. Remember, a stressed body must be allowed time for recovery and growth. Rest is essential.

This doesn't mean, however, that you should be inactive on the other days. On rest days, I walk for about an hour, sometimes in one long session, but usually broken up into two or three shorter sessions.

As I point out in *Ripped 2,* walking comes about as close as anything can to being a purely fat-burning activity. Perhaps just as importantly, when done at a comfortable pace, it doesn't break down muscle tissue or wear you out. Actually, it helps get rid of the fatigue by-products of exercise and speeds recovery.

The second guideline — distribute the aerobic stress to different parts of the body — is closely related to the first; it also prevents overtraining on aerobics by dovetailing aerobic and weight sessions. Here's how.

I work the same body parts aerobically and with weights. I have several aerobic exercise devices which allow me to do this: a stationary bike, rowing machine, Schwinn Air-Dyne, cross-country ski machine and HeavyHands. Of course, the stationary bike stresses the legs, and the rowing machine stresses the upper body. The Schwinn Air-Dyne has a push-pull arm action that's synchronized with the pedals, so it allows you to stress both the upper and lower body. The ski machine also works the upper and lower body, because you use a ski-poling action with the apparatus. And HeavyHands, the light dumbbells designed by Dr. Leonard Schwartz for aerobic exercise, can be used to stress any part of the body, but tend to fatigue the shoulders and arms more than other body parts.

As I said, I use these aerobic devices to put the second guideline into practice. Usually it works like this: I use the Air-Dyne or ski

170

My guidelines are designed to allow enough aerobic exercise for fat-burning purposes without causing a loss of muscle. Don't forget to walk or do something else similar on rest days. *Photo by John Balik.*

machine on days when I train my whole body; on days when I work the upper back and chest, I use the Air-Dyne (remember the push-pull arm action I mentioned?) or the rower; the stationary bike, of course, is perfect for leg days; and HeavyHands or the Air-Dyne again (with its push-pull action) do the trick on shoulder and arm days.

As you can easily see, switching around in this manner keeps aerobic exercise from wearing out (or, in this case, wearing down) any one body part excessively. Moreover, rotating the stress of the aerobic exercise in unison with your weight workouts facilitates recovery from both forms of exercise. You're giving all the muscles sufficient recovery time.

The third, and last, guideline — incorporate high-intensity muscular bursts into your aerobic sessions — has a different purpose than the other two. It's designed to make the fast-twitch muscle fibers, i.e., the fibers that have the greatest capacity for hypertrophy, a part of aerobic sessions. This is to remind the body that you're a lifter — not a marathoner — who needs fast-twitch muscle fibers. In short, the idea is to use your fast-twitch fibers even when you're doing aerobics, so you won't lose them. As the saying goes, "Use it or you lose it."

While the purpose of the third guideline is different, like the others, it also ties into the rhythm of my weight training sessions. The length and intensity of the bursts vary according to my training phase. When I'm doing high reps with the weights during the endurance phase of my weight training, the bursts are up to five minutes in length. At the other extreme, during the strength phase, when I'm using low reps and heavy weights, the bursts are as short as 15 seconds, but much more intense. In other words, the bursts emphasize muscular endurance during the endurance phase and muscular strength during the strength phase.

Let me caution you here: Don't overdo these muscular bursts. Don't turn your aerobics into sprint sessions. That would defeat your purpose. Aerobic (with oxygen) exercise, or exercise where your heart rate remains below 80 percent of maximum, burns mainly fat. When you go above 80 percent, the exercise becomes anaerobic (without oxygen) and is fueled mainly by the carbohydrate (glycogen) stored in the muscles. It's important to stay in the

172

aerobic range most of the time so you'll burn your fat stores! Bursts which push your heart rate above 80 percent should be only a small part of each aerobic session.

To show you how this works, here's an example of a stationary bike session taken from my training diary during the strength-endurance phase. I've marked the bursts and rest intervals. In addition, to make it clear what's happening, I've also included my perceived level of effort. When the exertion is "moderately hard" or "hard," I'm using my fast-twitch fibers and moving out of the aerobic range. When the exertion level is "easy" or "comfortable" — not too easy, not too hard — I'm training aerobically. Here's the bike routine:

Time	Resistance	Effort
5 minutes	100 watts (warm-up)	very easy
5	150 (begin)	Easy
4	175 (first burst)	Comfortable
1	150 (rest interval)	Easy
3	200 (second burst)	Harder, but still comfortable
2	150 (rest interval)	Easy
2	225 (third burst)	Moderately hard
3	150 (rest interval)	Easy
1	250 (fourth burst)	Hard
4	150 (rest interval)	Easy
3/4	275 (fifth burst)	Hard
2	150 (rest interval)	Easy
1/2	300 (sixth burst)	Hard
1-3/4	150 (rest interval)	Easy
5	75 (cool-down)	Very easy

TOTAL: 30 minutes (excluding warm-up and cool-down).

As you can see, I started with five minutes of warm-up and ended with five minutes of cool-down. During the main part of the ride, I did six bursts where I increased the resistance and pedaled faster. The bursts comprised a little over one-third of the ride and ranged in duration from four minutes down to 30 seconds. For the

173

shorter bursts, I used more resistance. I rested between bursts by turning the resistance down, and these rests became longer as the bursts got harder. I pushed my heart rate above 80 percent during the harder bursts, but you'll note I stayed in the aerobic range for most of the session (this is important!). I burned mainly fat for all but about four minutes.

As mentioned, this session was done during my strength-endurance training phase. In the endurance phase, I place more emphasis on the longer, less intense bursts, and during the strength phase I work more on the short, hard bursts. In other words, I do long bursts to develop endurance during the endurance phase, long *and* short bursts during the endurance-strength phase, and short, hard bursts to build strength during the final phase.

To clarify how my stationary bike routine changes from phase to phase, here's a routine from the strength phase. You'll notice it emphasizes shorter, more intense bursts:

Time	Resistance
5 minutes	100 watts (warm-up)
5	150 (begin)
5	175
1	150
1	200 (burst)
1	150
1	225 (burst)
1	150
1	250 (burst)
3	150
1	250 (burst)
2	150
3/4	275 (burst)
2	150
1/2	300 (burst)
2	150
1/4	325 (burst)
2	150
1/2	300 (burst)
5	75 (cool-down)

TOTAL: 30 minutes (excluding warm-up and cool-down).

174

I love my Tunturi. It's a pleasure to ride. Don't make the mistake of buying a cheap bike that you won't enjoy using. It's also important to ride in a stimulating setting. I watch TV. Others listen to rock music. Do whatever turns you on, but do something. *Photo by Guy Appelman.*

175

And here's a bike routine from the endurance phase, emphasizing longer, less intense bursts:

Time	Resistance
5 minutes	100 watts (warm-up)
5	150
5	175
4	200 (burst)
1	150
3	225 (burst)
2	150
2	250 (burst)
3	150
5	200 (burst)
5	75 (cool-down)

TOTAL: 30 minutes (excluding warm-up and cool-down).

I follow this same pattern — long bursts during the endurance phase, long *and* short bursts during the strength-endurance phase, and short bursts during the strength phase — when using the ski machine and the other aerobic devices mentioned earlier. I realize, of course, that you may not have such a variety of aerobic devices at your disposal. If that's the case, there are a number of alternatives you can follow.

First, you can get good results by simply alternating running and biking, two activities which almost anyone can do. Running and biking are a good combination because they affect the body differently. Both activities, of course, involve the muscles of the lower body, but the points of stress are sufficiently different to make alternating between the two worthwhile. That's why runners often include biking — stationary or regular biking — in their training program; it spreads the stress and allows them to train more without breaking down. For bodybuilders, switching back and forth permits more fat-burning activity without traumatizing the body and interfering with weight workouts.

A good plan is to bike on leg days and run when you do upper-body workouts. In both cases, include several sprints — longer

My friend Bill Pearl keeps his body fat low with a combination of stationary biking and rowing. Doesn't he look great at 55? *Photo by Chris Lund.*

and slower during the endurance phase of your weight training, shorter and faster during the strength phase. This will remind your fast-twitch fibers that you want them to stick around. Remember, do your weight workouts first, and the aerobics afterwards. Personally, I lift in the morning and do aerobics in the evening. I recommend that you do it this way, too, if your schedule permits. If not, it's okay to do them both in the same session.

Of course, running and biking is not the only combination you can use. In fact, it would be better to include some upper-body aerobic exercise in your program (less trauma and more fat burning). A combination that accomplishes this nicely is biking and rowing. Bill Pearl, the four-time Mr. Universe winner who's still in superb shape at age 55, divides his aerobic exercise between these two activities — with very good results. If you decide on this combination, bike on leg-training days and row on upper-body days.

If you'd like to include upper-body exercise in your aerobics program, but can't see your way to purchasing more than one piece of equipment, I recommend the Schwinn Air-Dyne. It has a push-pull arm action synchronized with the pedals, giving you the option of working the upper body, lower body or both. This upper and lower body exercise capability fits in nicely with a bodybuilding split training program. Let's take a detailed look at how the Air-Dyne can be used in conjunction with the Three-Way Plus One Routine described earlier. We'll take it through all three training phases.

The overall scheme is logical and simple. On upper back and chest day (Day One), emphasize the push-pull arm action, because it works the lats and pecs. On leg day (Day Two), use the pedals only to stress the legs (equally important, rest the upper body completely). On shoulder and arm day (Day Three), emphasize the arm action again. And on the fourth training day (Day Six), which, you'll recall, is the gentle whole-body day, use the pedals and arm levers together, but take it easy.

Except for shifting the stress around to the various body parts being trained that day with the weights, the basic format duplicates that of the stationary bike routines given earlier. Again, excluding warm-up and cool-down, the sessions last about 30 minutes, and the bursts vary from phase to phase — long bursts during the endurance phase, long and short during the strength-endurance phase, and short during the strength phase.

You already know about the Air-Dyne's arm action/pedal synchronization. To understand the routines which follow, the other thing you need to know about the Air-Dyne is that it utilizes air resistance (as air passes through wind vanes on the wheel) to provide a wide range of work loads. The faster the wheel is turned by the pedals and arm levers, the greater the air resistance and the amount of work required to move it. The Air-Dyne is equipped with a work-load indicator which shows how fast/hard you're working. The indicator goes from .5 (very easy) up to 7.0 (very hard). According to the instruction manual, at .5 you burn about three calories per minute and at 7.0 about 23. So, theroetically, you could burn up to 690 calories in a 30-minute session.

Now let's look at the Air-Dyne routines. On Day One, upper back and chest day, during the strength-endurance phase, your Air-Dyne session would look like this:

Time	Arms/Legs	Load
5 minutes	Arms & Legs	2.0 (Warm-Up)
5	Arms & Legs	3.0
5	Arms & Legs	4.0
2	Arms Only	2.5 (Burst)
2	Arms & Legs	3.5
1-1/2	Arms Only	3.0 (Burst)
2	Arms & Legs	3.5
1	Arms Only	3.5 (Burst)
2	Arms & Legs	3.5
1	Arms Only	3.5 (Burst)
2	Arms & Legs	3.5
1/2	Arms Only	4.0 (Burst)
2	Arms & Legs	3.5
1/4	Arms Only	4.5 (Burst)
1-1/2	Arms & Legs	3.5
1/4	Arms Only	4.5 (Burst)
1	Arms & Legs	5.0

1	Arms & Legs	4.0
1	Arms & Legs	6.0
1	Arms & Legs	3.0
1	Arms & Legs	5.5
5	Arms & Legs	2.0 (Cool-Down)

TOTAL: 30 minutes (excluding warm-up and cool-down).

At first glance, this may look complicated, but it isn't really. You're using the same basic pattern as in the stationary bike routine earlier: the initial bursts are long, and they get shorter as the intensity increases. The difference is that the bursts here are done with the arms only. While the arms and legs are used together most of the time in this routine (because you burn more calories by exercising both arms and legs), the emphasis is on the push-pull arm action, which works the upper back and chest. Note that the arms are used throughout the session.

Remember, this is the day you work your upper back and chest with the weights. Compared to the arms-only segments, the arm-and-leg segments in this routine are relatively easy. Again, that's because the emphasis is on the upper back and chest, not the legs. The legs are worked, yes, but not so hard they'll be depleted when you do the Squats and other leg exercises the next day.

This routine is repeated on Day Three, shoulder and arm day, but at about 15 percent less intensity. Simply scale the work load back by about .5 all the way through the routine. For example, on the first arms-only burst, drop the work load from 2.5 to 2.0. The effect is to stress the arms and shoulders again, but with less intensity. As with weights, aerobic exercise works best for body-building when you don't stress one part of your body hard more than once a week. The second aerobic training session for the same body parts should be done with less intensity.

On Day Two, leg training day, rest the arms completely, and work the legs aerobically, using the pedals only. Sit back, rest your hands on your thighs and pedal like you would riding a bike ("Look, ma, no hands!"). As in the stationary bike routine given earlier, start with longer, easier bursts, and then gradually shorten the length of the bursts and increase the intensity.

180

The Schwinn Air-Dyne, shown here, is probably my favorite aerobic exercise device. The push-pull arm action allows you to spread the stress of aerobic exercise over practically the entire body. You can work your arms and legs together or separately. *Photo by Guy Appelman.*

The Nordic Track ski machine is another excellent whole-body aerobic exercise device. It stresses the body differently than the Air-Dyne. It really works the large calorie-burning muscles in the hips and lower back. *Photo by Guy Appelman.*

Finally, on Day Six, the day you train the whole body with weights, follow the stationary bike routine format again (as you did on Day Two), but use your legs *and* arms together the entire session. If you use the Air-Dyne at the same work-load level you did on leg day, the effort will be relatively easy, because your legs will now be getting help from the arms.

In summary, the emphasis is on the push-pull arm action when you train your upper back and chest on Day One, and when you train shoulders and arms on Day Three. On leg day, work only your lower body by pedaling with your hands free. Use arms and legs together on Day Six, when you train your whole body with the weights, but keep the intensity low to match the intensity of the weight workout on that day. You see, the aerobic training pattern using the Air-Dyne really is logical and simple.

The Air-Dyne routines we've discussed up to now are for the strength-endurance phase of training (the middle phase). As we mentioned earlier, during the endurance phase, which leads off the cycle, do longer bursts and use lower training loads. And during the strength phase, which concludes the cycle, emphasize shorter bursts and use more resistance.

To make sure there's no confusion, here's an example of an Air-Dyne routine with emphasis on the arms for use during the *endurance* phase. Note that the arms-only bursts are relatively long — two minutes.

Time	Arms/Legs	Load
5 minutes	Arms & Legs	2.0 (Warm-Up)
5	Arms & Legs	3.0
5	Arms & Legs	4.0
2	Arms Only	2.0 (Burst)
2	Arms & Legs	3.5
2	Arms Only	2.5 (Burst)
2	Arms & Legs	3.5
2	Arms Only	3.0 (Burst)
2	Arms & Legs	3.5
2	Arms Only	2.5 (Burst)
1	Arms & Legs	5.0
1	Arms & Legs	4.0

1	Arms & Legs	6.0
1	Arms & Legs	3.0
1	Arms & Legs	4.0
1	Arms & Legs	5.0
5	Arms & Legs	2.0 (Cool-Down)

TOTAL: 30 minutes (excluding warm-up and cool-down).

Here's an example of an Air-Dyne routine with emphasis on the arms for use during the *strength* phase of training. Note that the arms-only bursts are shorter and more intense than they were during the endurance phase. They range in duration from one minute down to 15 seconds.

Time	Arms/Legs	Load
5 minutes	Arms & Legs	2.0 (Warm-Up)
5	Arms & Legs	3.0
5	Arms & Legs	4.0
1	Arms Only	3.0 (Burst)
2	Arms & Legs	3.5
1	Arms Only	3.5 (Burst)
2	Arms & Legs	3.5
1/2	Arms Only	4.0 (Burst)
2	Arms & Legs	3.5
1/2	Arms Only	4.0 (Burst)
2	Arms & Legs	3.5
1/4	Arms Only	4.5 (Burst)
1-3/4	Arms & Legs	3.5
1/4	Arms Only	4.5 (Burst)
1-3/4	Arms & Legs	3.5
1	Arms & Legs	5.0
1	Arms & Legs	4.0
1	Arms & Legs	6.0
1	Arms & Legs	3.0
1	Arms & Legs	5.5
5	Arms & Legs	2.0 (Cool-Down)

TOTAL: 30 minutes (excluding warm-up and cool-down).

Here's a second arm-emphasis Air-Dyne routine for the strength phase. One of my favorites, it keeps you moving at a substantial pace and has lots of variety.

Time	Arms/Legs	Load
5 minutes	Arms & Legs	2.0 (Warm-Up)
5	Arms & Legs	3.0
5	Arms & Legs	4.0
1/2	Arms Only	3.0 (Burst)
1	Arms & Legs	4.0
1/2	Arms Only	3.5 (Burst)
1	Arms & Legs	4.0
1/2	Arms & Legs	3.0 (Burst)
1	Arms & Legs	4.0
1/2	Arms Only	3.5 (Burst)
1	Arms & Legs	5.0
1	Arms & Legs	3.0
1	Arms & Legs	5.0
1	Arms & Legs	3.0
1	Arms & Legs	5.0
1/4	Arms Only	4.0 (Burst)
1	Arms & Legs	4.0
1/4	Arms Only	4.5 (Burst)
1	Arms & Legs	4.0
1/4	Arms Only	4.0 (Burst)
1	Arms & Legs	4.0
1/4	Arms Only	4.5 (Burst)
1	Arms & Legs	4.0
1	Arms & Legs	5.0
1	Arms & Legs	6.0
1	Arms & Legs	3.5
1	Arms & Legs	5.5
5	Arms & Legs	2.0 (Cool-Down)

TOTAL: 30 minutes (excluding warm-up and cool-down).

Please note that the work loads in this and the other sample routines are the ones I use; they're geared to my capacities. If you choose to work out on the Air-Dyne, you'll probably require higher or lower work loads. Experiment to find the loads best suited to your needs. (If you're not in shape, start slowly and build up gradually as your condition improves.) Make the bursts hard enough to activate your fast-twitch fibers, but don't overdo it. Reserve your highest intensity for weight workouts. It's rarely a good idea to push aerobic sessions to the point where they're no longer fun.

Remember, bursts are not meant to *build* muscle — you do that with the weights. Their purpose is to *maintain* muscle tissue. They activate your fast-twitch fibers during aerobic sessions so you won't lose them. Plus, bursts provide variety and interest, taking the boredom out of aerobic exercise. They're meant to be fun.

Finally, to give you the big picture in condensed form, here's a chart showing how weight and Air-Dyne routines fit together on the Three-Way Plus One Split:

DAY ONE:
Morning: Weight training (upper back and chest) — hard
Evening: Air-Dyne with upper body emphasis — hard

DAY TWO:
Morning: Weight training (legs) — hard
Evening: Air-Dyne — pedals only — hard

DAY THREE:
Morning: Weight training (arms and shoulders) — hard
Evening: Air-Dyne with upper body emphasis — moderate

DAY FOUR:
Rest day — walk

DAY FIVE:
Rest day — walk

DAY SIX:
Morning: Weight training (whole body) — easy
Evening: Air-Dyne using arms and legs together — easy

DAY SEVEN:
Rest day — walk

Best of luck with your aerobics. Remember, make it fun!

Boyer Coe, pictured here, has probably won more national and world level bodybuilding contests than any other person. We correspond occasionally, and I recommended in one of my letters that he try the Nordic Track. He did and liked it. A short time later, he wrote: "And you're right, you do sweat buckets, in my case it's more like wash tubs!"

I guess that proves we're all a little different. So be sure to adjust the aerobic routines to suit your own capacities. And remember, make it fun! *Photo by Chris Lund.*

ADVICE ON STRETCHING

It's beyond the scope of this book to discuss stretching in detail. But some comments are in order, because many people stretch at the wrong time or for the wrong reasons. Thus, they do more harm than good.

The problem is that often people don't know why they stretch. The reason for stretching is to increase range of motion and prevent injuries. Unfortunately, many people have the idea that stretching is a good way to warm up. That's wrong. In fact, stretching should be done only *after* you are warmed up. Stretching before warming up is an invitation to injury.

According to a recent report in *The Physician and Sportsmedicine* (March 1986), stretching before your body has been warmed up is dangerous because it can damage connective tissues in the joints; the collagen may undergo a type of plastic deformation. In addition, there's a higher friction force in the muscles when they're cold. A cold muscle, like a cold rubber band, simply isn't ready to be stretched.

A warm-up increases the elasticity of the tendons and ligaments and causes a rise in the temperature of the muscle cells; this prepares the body to exercise or stretch. Sportsmedicine doctors recommend stretching only after a warm-up in which body temperature is increased slightly (to the point of perspiration) and the muscles are warm and pliable.

Dr. Stan James, the orthopedic surgeon who operated on Joan Benoit's knee a few months before her victory in the 1984 Olympic marathon, recommends that athletes stretch after their workouts — not before — when their muscles are warm. That's what I do.

I usually stretch immediately after my aerobic sessions. Stretching is a relatively recent addition to my training program. I began doing it regularly about a year ago, and I believe I have fewer muscle and joint strains as a result. The added flexibility probably protects me against injury. Plus, I enjoy stretching; it feels good. If done properly, it's a good way to wind down and relax.

Stretching should be slow and sustained, not fast, forceful, and jerky. Bob Anderson, whose book *Stretching* (Shelter Publications, 1980) has sold more than 500,000 copies, says that the proper way to stretch is to do it *painlessly*. If you stretch to the point of pain, you're doing it wrong.

Anderson also says that drastic stretching and jerky, bouncy, ballistic-type stretching can cause injury and actually promote inflexibility; it creates little tears in the muscle fibers, which lead to the formation of scar tissue and a gradual loss of elasticity. He recommends that you stretch slowly and easily to a point where you feel mild tension; at that point, relax and hold the stretch. The feeling of tension should subside as you hold the position. If it feels uncomfortable, and especially if you feel pain, ease off.

For more information on stretching, I recommend that you read Bob Anderson's book. It contains stretching routines for weight training and many other activities. Anderson can also supply you with stretching charts to put on the wall.

Remember, stretch only after you're warmed up. Don't do forceful, jerky movements or stretch to the point that it hurts.

Stretching should feel good. If it hurts, you're doing it wrong. *Photo by Guy Appelman.*

ABOUT MY OTHER BOOKS

By now you've probably got the idea, but just in case you haven't, I'll say it flat out: You should read *Ripped, Ripped 2* and *The Lean Advantage.* This book focuses on what I've learned since writing those books. It doesn't replace them. It builds on and adds to them. Many important concepts fully developed in my other books are only touched on here. Others are left out entirely.

My first book, *RIPPED: The Sensible Way to Achieve Ultimate Muscularity,* was published in 1980. Now in its fifth printing, it continues to be a best-seller. When people call and ask about the books, I always tell them to read *Ripped* first. It contains the story of my first reduction to 2.4 percent body fat and my wins at the Past-40 Mr. America and Mr. USA contests. It tells how my now decade-long study of losing fat and gaining muscle began. It details the critical role played by body composition tests in the formulation of my overall philosophy. Most importantly, however, *Ripped* details the thinking process — the mistakes and successes — which led to the underlying principles of my diet and training program. That's significant, because it's the same trial-and-error process you'll go through to solve your own special problems. In short, *Ripped* is the basic book in the series. All my other books spring from it.

I've already made reference to the crucially important sections in *Ripped 2* on The Hard/Easy Training Principle, Coaxing Long-Term Gains and The Importance of Rest. But there are other key sections in *Ripped 2,* such as All Or None (the all-or-none law of muscle fiber contraction), The Meaning of Intensity, High-Intensity Training Techniques, Coping with Calories, The Famine Phenomenon, and Muscle-Building Nutrition.

In *Ripped 2,* I introduce you to variable training intensity, which is the most important feature of the training routines in the book. Those routines focus on developing the contractile fibers; therefore, they're the foundation for the more sophisticated routines in this book.

I've also referred to *The Lean Advantage* a number of times in this book. It's a compilation of the first four years of my monthly column on losing fat and gaining muscle in *Muscle & Fitness*

If you call Ripped Enterprises, the first person you'll talk to will probably be my wife, Carol. As you know, I dedicated this book to her. *Photo by Guy Appelman.*

magazine. The topics covered by the nearly 50 "Ripped" columns written during that time are organized under 16 different chapter headings. As you probably know, my column gives answers to questions asked by readers from all walks of life and all parts of the country. Some of their concerns are the same as yours; others, equally important, may never have occurred to you. Many topics not included or fully developed in the other books are addressed in *The Lean Advantage.* Here are some of the topic headings:

You Need Dietary Fat
New Evidence on Protein Needs
Alcohol and Weight Control
The Problem With Training to Failure
Home vs. Gym Training
Stationary Biking For Bodybuilders
HeavyHands: Four Limbs Are Better Than Two
Two-Day Lag Rule
Inspiration
Curing Burnout
Fear of Fat
Leanness and Lifespan
Loose Skin
A Nation of Fatties
Advice on Advice
Aerobics Can Lower Your Body Fat Setpoint

And *The Lean Advantage* has lots more! One of the most popular chapters in the book is on a subject of interest to almost everyone: developing a well-defined waistline.

Again, I recommend that you read my other books. After all, you wouldn't expect to benefit fully from an advanced course in creative writing without first taking English 101, would you?

I'm sure you get my point.

FINAL REMINDERS

On Diet:

1. Don't lose more than one pound a week. If you try to lose faster, you'll lose muscle and probably go off your diet as well.

2. Don't completely eliminate fattening foods such as peanut butter from your diet. If you do, you'll feel deprived and probably end up binging.

3. Don't stop eating bread, potatoes and pasta; they satisfy your appetite without making you fat.

4. Eat a lot of fruit and vegetables; they fill you up without filling you out.

5. Use meat primarily as a flavoring agent, not as a main course.

6. Don't eat haphazardly; uniform eating helps you keep track of your caloric intake.

7. Don't skip meals. Regular eating — three meals plus snacks — makes it less likely that you'll overeat.

8. Choose white fish over the darker varieties of fish, because white fish is lower in fat and calories. Stick with the white meat of poultry as well, and don't eat the fat-laden skin.

9. Don't frequent fast-food or all-you-can-eat restaurants. Why tempt yourself needlessly?

10. Don't order fancy dishes when you eat out. By sticking to dishes that are plain and simple, you'll know whether you're getting added fat or sugar.

On Training:

1. Don't train with maximum intensity every workout. Do each exercise hard once each week and with less intensity the second time.

2. Don't begin a new training period with very heavy weights. Start with comfortable poundages and pace yourself to a new personal record at the end of each periodization phase.

3. Don't miss a single rep by pushing yourself to failure. Gradually increase training poundages, building confidence for the next workout. Focus on success.

4. Workouts should last about an hour (90 minutes at most). Train longer and your concentration and intensity will suffer.

5. Don't allow training to become a bore; make variety the keystone of your program.

6. Don't overdo aerobic exercise; 30 minutes four times a week is plenty. Have fun!

7. Don't stretch unless you're warmed up; take it slow and easy — never bounce or make it hurt.

8. Don't plunge into an exercise program — weights or aerobics — if you haven't been training regularly. Start slowly and build up gradually as your condition improves.

9. Don't neglect Squats and Deadlifts. They're hard, but they make your whole body grow.

10. Give periodization a sincere try. It's simply the best way to train. □

Well, that's it for now. But I'll be back. Until then, good training. *Photo by John Balik.*

HAVE YOU READ CLARENCE BASS' OTHER BOOKS?

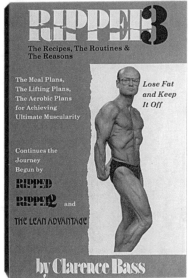

The three *Ripped* books are the bodybuilding series. They cover all aspects of gaining maximum muscle with minimm fat. (See page 190 and following for more details.)

Clarence Bass' **RIPPED**™ Enterprises
528 Chama N.E., Albuquerque, New Mexico 87108
Phone: 505-266-5858 • Fax: 505-266-9123
E-mail: cncbass@aol.com • Web site: http://www.cbass.com

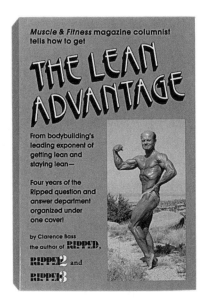

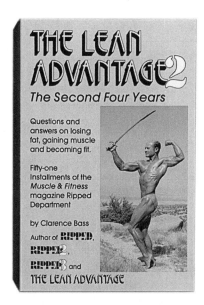

The **Lean Advantage** series is in question and answer form. The three books are a compilation of more than 12 years of Clarence Bass' column, "The Ripped Department" in *Muscle & Fitness* magazine. If you have questions about losing fat, getting fit, healthy lifestyle, aging or anything relating to diet and exercise, the answers are here. (See page 190 and following for more details.)

Clarence Bass' RIPPED™ Enterprises
528 Chama N.E., Albuquerque, New Mexico 87108
Phone: 505-266-5858 • Fax: 505-266-9123
E-mail: cncbass@aol.com • Web site: http://www.cbass.com

In *Lean For Life*, Clarence Bass presents a three-pronged fitness and fat loss program: diet, aerobics and weights. But it's much more than that. It's a psychologically sound plan for permanent leanness. It's an enjoyable eating style; you always leave the table feeling full and satisfied. It's a balanced exercise program—strength and endurance—which is structured for success; positive feedback keeps you motivated. In short, it's a lifestyle approach that will make you lean for life!

Clarence Bass' **RIPPED**™ Enterprises
528 Chama N.E., Albuquerque, New Mexico 87108
Phone: 505-266-5858 • Fax: 505-266-9123
E-mail: cncbass@aol.com • Web site: http://www.cbass.com

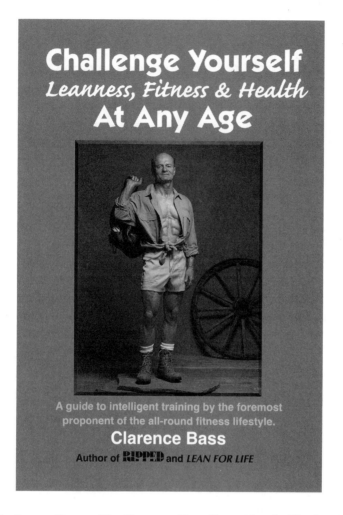

Challenge Yourself
Leanness, Fitness & Health
At Any Age

A guide to intelligent training by the foremost proponent of the all-round fitness lifestyle.

Clarence Bass

Author of RIPPED and *LEAN FOR LIFE*

Challenge Yourself is Clarence Bass' latest book. The key to becoming—and staying— lean, fit and healthy is to continually challenge yourself in an intelligent and thoughtful way. That's what this book is about. It explains how Clarence has continued to improve for more than 45 years—and how you can follow suit. The other books get you started and this book will keep you going.

Cutting edge, ***Challenge Yourself*** includes psychologically sound techniques for staying motivated, the latest developments in diet and nutrition, detailed new routines for beginners and intermediates (weights only), Clarence's current routine, athlete-type strength training, high-intensity aerobics, longevity and health topics, and exciting personal profiles.

Please visit us at http://www.cbass.com

You'll find not only information about our books and other products, but also more about Clarence Bass' background and training career, his diet and training philosophy in brief, frequently asked questions, late news — and new articles by Clarence Bass (a new article at the beginning of each month). We are your source for bodybuilding, fitness, health, motivation, diet and fat loss information

Also available from
Clarence Bass'
RIPPED Enterprises

- ❖ Posing Trunks
- ❖ Women's Posing Suits
- ❖ Audio Tapes
- ❖ Videos
- ❖ Color Photos
- ❖ Food Supplements
- ❖ Selected Books
- ❖ Personal Consultations

Model: Dorine Tilton